Military Assistance
in Recent Wars

THE WASHINGTON PAPERS

. . . intended to meet the need for an authoritative, yet prompt, public appraisal of the major developments in world affairs.

Series Editors: Walter Laqueur; Amos A. Jordan

Associate Editors: William J. Taylor, Jr.; M. Jon Vondracek

Executive Editor: Jean C. Newsom

Managing Editor: Nancy B. Eddy

Editorial Assistant: Ann E. Ellsworth

President, CSIS: Amos A. Jordan

MANUSCRIPT SUBMISSION

The Washington Papers and Praeger Publishers welcome inquiries concerning manuscript submissions. Please include with your inquiry a curriculum vita, synopsis, table of contents, and estimated manuscript length. Manuscripts must be between 120–200 double-spaced typed pages. All submissions will be peer reviewed. Submissions to *The Washington Papers* should be sent to *The Washington Papers*; The Center for Strategic and International Studies; Georgetown University; 1800 K Street NW; Suite 400; Washington, DC, 20006. Book proposals should be sent to Praeger Publishers; 521 Fifth Avenue; New York NY 10175.

The Washington Papers/122

Military Assistance in Recent Wars

The Dominance of the Superpowers

Stephanie G. Neuman

Foreword by Ernest Graves

Published with The Center for
Strategic and International Studies,
Georgetown University, Washington, D.C.

PRAEGER

New York
Westport, Connecticut
London

Library of Congress Cataloging-in-Publication Data

Neuman, Stephanie G.
  Military assistance in recent wars.

  (The Washington papers, ISSN 0278-937X; vol. XIV, 122)
  "Published with the Center for Strategic and
International Studies, Georgetown University,
Washington, D.C."
  1. Munitions. 2. Military assistance. 3. Military
history, Modern—20th century. 4. Developing countries
—History, Military. I. Georgetown University.
Center for Strategic and International Studies.
  II. Title. III. Series.
  UF530.N47 1986   355′.032   86-16911
  ISBN 0-275-92219-7 (alk. paper)
  ISBN 0-275-92220-0 (pbk.: alk. paper)

Library of Congress Catalog Card Number: 86-16911
ISBN: 0-275-92219-7 cloth   ISBN: 0-275-92220-0 paper

First published in 1986

Praeger Publishers, 521 Fifth Avenue, New York, NY 10175
A division of Greenwood Press, Inc.

Printed in the United States of America
∞
The paper used in this book complies with the Permanent
Paper Standard issued by the National Information Standards
Organization (Z39.48-1984).

10 9 8 7 6 5 4 3 2 1

Contents

Foreword

Despite four decades as the most powerful nation on earth, the United States still is not comfortable with its role as the leader of the free world. Americans do not like to have their security and economic well-being depend on developments in the farthest corners of the earth, and they do not like to see their government deeply involved in trying to influence the course of events in foreign countries, no matter how much this may be justified as necessary to protect their freedom and their way of life. Nevertheless, these are the imperatives U.S. citizens face, and the more we come to accept them, the better will be our chances of dealing effectively with the dangers and opportunities confronting the United States.

No small part of the problem lies in a dearth of knowledge and understanding of the workings of international politics and a natural fear of the unknown. In these circumstances the United States is fortunate to have a scholar of the caliber of Stephanie Neuman, working intensely in the field of international conflict, committed to revealing what counts and what does not count in resolving the disputes that rack the Third World.

Dr. Neuman's latest research focuses on an area of international security affairs that has not received enough attention: how and to what extent the suppliers of arms influence the outcome of hostilities in the Third World. Much greater attention has been paid to the trade in arms short of war and to ways to limit this trade and avoid its adverse consequences. As the present work makes abundantly clear, however, military assistance is a potent weapon of policy, used or withheld with great effect by the superpowers. Dependent as we are on developments around the world, it is vital to understand the uses of military assistance and to use this assistance wisely, whether in the U.S. rivalry with the Soviet Union or in other conflicts damaging to U.S. interests in a stable, productive world.

Foreign assistance, particularly military assistance, involves many subtleties and complexities. It is highly political. Some decry this situation, arguing that the United States often gets very little return for its grants and loans, which, in the case of military assistance, may aggravate an already dangerous situation. Dr. Neuman's research indicates otherwise. Her examination of eight recent wars shows that both the Soviet Union and the United States are intent on using military assistance not only to advance their interests in the Third World, but also to prevent any of the conflicts there from escalating to the point at which open hostilities between the two superpowers might occur. The United States also can use foreign assistance to gain an advantage in its competition with the Soviet Union. This book describes one of the important ways in which this is being done.

The wealth of information and the careful analysis in the pages that follow provide abundant food for thought. The author's insights contain valuable lessons for policymakers and the public alike. Both can expect to gain a fresh appreciation of the role of military assistance in dealing with an often dangerous world.

Ernest Graves
Former Director, Defense Security Assistance Agency
Senior Fellow in International Security Studies, CSIS

Preface

The idea for this book was conceived four years ago when Robert Harkavy and I were discussing the possibility of organizing a large study on the lessons from recent wars. In mapping out the dimensions of the project, it was only logical, given my research interests, that a comparative analysis of both the role of military assistance and Third World military industries be included. The more we talked the more interesting the prospect grew. Much appears in the press and academic literature about particular wars and specific arms transfers to the combatants, but because there has been little or no comparative research on the subject, there are few guidelines available to help assess whether what is described is idiosyncratic or symptomatic of general trends in the international system. This paper, then, represents an effort to make some larger sense out of the myriad individual military-related transfers to combatants in recent wars and to understand how these transactions are connected to political and economic developments in the international system as a whole. I am grateful to the Department of Defense, which supported a part of the research.

Written between 1983 and 1986, this book grew from its original concept as a short chapter in a symposium volume on lessons of recent wars to its present length and organization.* As I searched for and found new material, I faced fresh questions that demanded still further thought and investigation. Unhappily, I found there is an inverse relationship between the interest of the question and the amount of information available about it. Because much of the data on arms transfers is classified, I was forced to search public sources for bits of information, which then had to be pieced together into a larger, intelligible whole. The task was painstaking and time-consuming, sometimes frustrating but also often very rewarding.

In my quest for data and greater meaning, I was assisted by a host of informants in Washington who gave liberally of their time. They made the job of data collection and interpretation easier by generously sharing their ideas and expertise with me. I am particularly indebted to Morton S. Miller, Department of State, who was always ready to offer suggestions, discuss and debate, and to steer me to others in the Department of State who might have another opinion. I also drew remorselessly on the resources of The Defense Security Assistance Agency (DSAA) and the Arms Control and Disarmament Agency (ACDA). Judy Frey (DSAA) and Dan Gallik (ACDA) always dealt with my many queries with great patience, diligence, and good humor. Without their assistance and that of Harry Zubkoff, Department of Defense, who generously opened his files of press clippings to me, data collection would have been immeasureably more difficult. I am also grateful to Dr. Dov Zakheim of the Department of Defense and Dr. Andrew Semmel, now on the staff of the Senate Foreign Relations Committee but then an analyst for the DSAA, who took the time to read and offer valuable comments on one of the many versions of this manuscript.

Much of the research and all of the writing were done at

---

*Parts of chapter 2 appear in *The Lessons of Recent Wars in the Third World: Comparative Dimensions*, vol. II (Lexington, Mass.: Lexington Books, 1986), which I coedited with Robert Harkavy.

the Research Institute for International Change at Columbia University. Over the past three years, my thinking about the role of military aid in recent wars has benefited greatly from the insights and help of my colleagues and students. Robert Jervis and Elizabeth Valkenier read an earlier draft of this manuscript in whole or in part and encouraged me with their comments to continue developing it. Elliot Zupnick was always ready when asked to give of his mathematical expertise and knowledge about international trade. And my students contributed, perhaps unknowingly, to the development of my ideas with the questions they asked and their responses to those I raised in class. Dawit Toga, my research assistant for much of this period, tirelessly gathered data and provided computational assistance under conditions that were not always easy. His efforts are greatly appreciated. Leonard Kreyin, who succeeded him, gave of his intelligence and unflagging energy with good humor during the production phase of this manuscript. In addition, I derived a great deal from the suggestions of the two readers of the manuscript, who were always constructive in their criticism.

Above all, however, I owe much to my friend and colleague Robert Harkavy, who read, commented on, and supported my efforts from the very beginning.

Finally, a vote of thanks to my husband, who has accepted the inconvenience of not having a traditional wife. This effort would have been impossible without his cooperation and encouragement.

I am profoundly indebted to all these institutions and individuals for their support, advice, and assistance. But in the final analysis, only I can be held responsible for the material and arguments presented here – and for their errors and deficiencies.

Columbia University
June 13, 1986

About the Author

Stephanie Neuman is a senior research scholar at the Research Institute on International Change and director of its Comparative Defense Studies Program at Columbia University. She has been at Columbia since 1976, researching and teaching about Third World security issues. Prior to that, Dr. Neuman taught international relations and comparative foreign policy at The Graduate Faculty of the New School for Social Research. In recent years she has traveled widely in the Middle East and Asia, lecturing in Israel, Iran, Thailand, South Korea, and Australia.

Her recent publications include "The Arms Trade in Recent Wars: The Role of the Superpowers" (*International Affairs*, Summer 1986); *The Lessons of Recent Wars*, vols. I and II, contributor and coeditor with Robert E. Harkavy (Lexington Books, 1985 and 1986); "Offsets in the International Arms Market," in *World Military Expenditures and Arms Transfers, 1985* (U.S. Arms Control and Disarmament Agency); "Coproduction, Barter, and Countertrade: Offsets in the International Arms Market," *Orbis* (Spring 1985); "Arms Production in Taiwan" (with A. James Gregor and Robert E. Harkavy) in Stockholm International Peace Research Institute, *Arms Production in the Third World: A Factual Survey* (Taylor and Francis, 1985); *Defense Planning in Less In-*

dustrialized States: The Middle East and South Asia, editor and contributor (Lexington Books, 1984); "International Stratification and Third World Military Industries," *International Organization* (Winter 1984); "The Arms Trade and U.S. National Interests," in *Power and Politics in Transition*, Vojtech Mastny, ed. (Greenwood Press, 1984); "Third World Military Industries and the Arms Trade," in *Arms Production in Developing Countries: An Analysis of Decision-Making*, James E. Katz, ed. (Lexington Books, 1984); and "Israeli Defense Industries" (coauthored with Robert E. Harkavy) in *Arms Production in Developing Countries: An Analysis of Decision-Making* (Lexington Books, 1984).

To my husband, Herbert.

1

Introduction

A Question of Focus

Armed conflict has become endemic in the Third World. Some analysts believe that these conflicts indicate a decline in the power of the major states because of their inability to prevent the outbreak of violence or limit its intensity.[1] The rising number of weapon suppliers, particularly the growing capabilities of Third World countries to produce and transfer arms, is noted with special concern and alarm. According to these analysts, the general availability of weapons not only promotes armed conflict, it also indicates that the major powers have suffered a relative loss of control over the international system.[2] Thus, in their view, the very existence of new suppliers has negative implications for the structure of the international system and the role of the superpowers in it. As one U.S. government agency warns,

> The introduction of new, more potent weapons heightens the possibility of conflict while reducing the ability of the major powers to limit the intensity of potential warfare.[3]

And another study concludes:

1

> The diffusion of defense capabilities contributes . . . to the erosion of the early postwar system of imperial or hegemonic roles formerly played by the major powers around the globe. Thus the superpowers, and even the medium-sized powers such as Britain and France, are losing the ability to "control" or influence events in their former colonies or zones of special influence.[4]

This paper attempts to test these assumptions by examining the role security assistance has played in recent wars. It focuses on the activities of the combatants and their suppliers in an effort to assess how the global arms trade actually functions during periods of armed conflict. I address three general questions: What kind of military assistance did the combatants receive and from whom? How did this assistance affect the operations and outcome of the wars? What are the implications for the structure of the international system and the role of the superpowers in this system?

A Sample of Wars

Eight recent wars – five conventional interstate wars and three wars involving insurgencies – form the data base for this study:

Conventional Wars

Ethiopia/Somalia (The Horn)
Vietnam/The People's Republic of China (PRC)
Iran/Iraq (The Gulf)
Argentina/Great Britain (The Falklands)
Israel/Syria/The Palestine Liberation Organization (PLO)
   (Lebanon)

Insurgencies

Morocco/Polisario (The Western Sahara)
El Salvador/Honduras/Nicaragua/The Contras
   (Central America)
Afghanistan/USSR/The Afghan Rebels

The duration of these wars varies widely. Spanning the years 1977 to 1985, some are still in progress while others lasted less than a month. (See table 1.) Whether long or short, ongoing or terminated, conventional or unconventional, however, a common factor in all these recent engagements is the unresolved nature of the original dispute and the continuing threat of new armed hostilities. In Southeast Asia, Vietnam and China continue to skirmish on their borders; tension and occasional outbursts characterize Somali-Ethiopian relations in the Horn; Argentine irredentist frustration over the Falklands still simmers; and in Lebanon violence has not abated. The different impacts of these wars on patterns of military assistance and the role played by the superpowers are the central themes addressed in this section.

A Model of Arms Supply Relationships[5]

Four basic arms supply patterns have characterized supplier-recipient relationships during recent wars. (See table 2.)

Internal Transfers

Countries with extensive indigenous defense industries that are only moderately dependent on external sources of supply fall into this category. For the most part, their own defense industries supply the arms. Note that only one less developed country (LDC) combatant, China, falls into this category, although other countries, such as Israel and Argentina, have varying levels of military production capability.

Bilateral Government-to-Government Agreements

References to the arms trade in the general literature are usually made in this context. These agreements include all legally binding understandings between the governments of sovereign states for the sale or gift of military equipment and related services. Recipients may choose to obtain arms princi-

TABLE 1
Sequence and Duration of Recent Wars

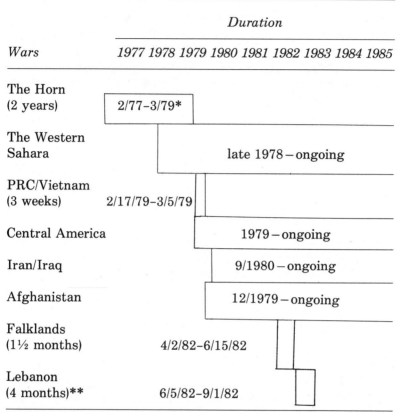

Wars	Duration								
	1977	1978	1979	1980	1981	1982	1983	1984	1985
The Horn (2 years)	2/77–3/79*								
The Western Sahara			late 1978 – ongoing						
PRC/Vietnam (3 weeks)	2/17/79–3/5/79								
Central America			1979 – ongoing						
Iran/Iraq				9/1980 – ongoing					
Afghanistan			12/1979 – ongoing						
Falklands (1½ months)			4/2/82–6/15/82						
Lebanon (4 months)**			6/5/82–9/1/82						

*Because of the ongoing nature of conflict in the Third World, it is often difficult to establish exactly when recent wars began and when they ended. For example, three different dates are commonly used to mark the onset of the Horn War: 2/77 – the first independent report of fighting in the Ogaden; 6/77 – the first official Ethiopian accusation that Somalian regular troops were involved; and 7/77 – the first confirmation by Somalian officials that "volunteer Somalian troops" were fighting in the Ogaden. For the purposes of this study, February 1977, when the first tank skirmishes were reported, is used to designate the beginning of the war.

**The war termination date used here is the day the PLO withdrew its forces from Lebanon. That date would not be acceptable to the PLO, which claims its war against Israel continues. Because the major military transfers involved Syria and Israel, the Lebanon conflict is treated here as an interstate war and the unofficial cessation of armed hostilities between Syria and Israel as the war termination date.

TABLE 2
LDC Patterns of Resupply During War

Type of War	Internal	Bilateral	Indirect	Restricted
Conventional	PRC	Vietnam		Argentina
		Syria		
		Israel	Iraq	Iran
		Ethiopia		Somalia
Insurgencies		Afghanistan		Afghan rebels
			Morocco	Polisario
			Honduras	Contras
			El Salvador	
			Nicaragua	

pally from one supplier, or they may decide to procure weapons from a number of sources.

A study by Amelia Leiss et al. presents a typology of five government-to-government arms supply relationships.[6] Because the number of combatants analyzed here is so small, however, I merged Leiss's five categories into two basic transfer patterns: Monopoly/Principal, in which one supplier provides 50 percent or more of an LDC's military assistance, and Diversified/Multiple, in which two suppliers each contribute 45 percent or more of a country's military assistance or three or more donors are involved, none of which provide more than 49 percent of a recipient's military assistance.

In this study, ten of the combatants obtained their resupply primarily through bilateral agreements with another government. Eight of these states dealt with one of the superpowers. Ethiopia, Afghanistan, Vietnam, Syria, and Nicaragua procured weapons from the Soviet Union, while Israel, Honduras, and El Salvador obtained supplies from the United States. Iraq and Morocco have received a large proportion of their military equipment through bilateral arrangements with other governments as well. (See table 2 and appendix 1.)

Indirect Transfers

Third-party sales, whereby equipment or services provided by one government to another government are transferred by the latter to a third government or insurgent force, are included in this category, along with other nongovernment sources of military equipment such as the private arms trade. Iran, Argentina, Somalia, and insurgent forces, all subject to embargoes during wartime, have resorted mainly to indirect sources, while Iraq, Morocco, Nicaragua, Honduras, and El Salvador have received assistance from indirect sources as well as from principal government suppliers.

Another form of indirect transfer occurs when one country acts as a surrogate or proxy supplier for another. It is often difficult, however, to distinguish between this type of indirect transfer and direct bilateral government agreements. Given the sensitivities of the parties involved, particularly during wartime, both suppliers and recipients often have a stake in concealing whether a donor government is acting independently or in cooperation with another power. Throughout this study, the distinction between direct and indirect bilateral assistance has been made wherever possible.

Restricted Arms Transfers

This category covers what one might call "negative transfers." It includes embargoes, political restrictions, and the inability or unwillingness of a supplier to provide certain military technologies or services to a combatant. Just as the availability of supplies has proven critical to a war's prosecution and outcome, so too has the inaccessibility of assistance. Because indirect transfers are generally a product of and associated with transfer restrictions implemented by one of the superpowers, they are discussed in tandem in this paper.

A Methodological Note

The term "security assistance" is used here synonymously with "military assistance" and "military aid" to describe the transfer of military equipment and/or training and other related services to another country, whether this is in the form of a sale, offset arrangement, or grant. Following the U.S. Arms Control and Disarmament Agency's usage, "military equipment" is defined as conventional "weapons of war, parts thereof, ammunition, support equipment, and other commodities considered primarily military in nature . . . Also included are transfers of equipment for defense industries."[7]

Unfortunately, in the following analysis, the definition of security assistance may be more rigorous than the data supporting it. The dollar values used below were obtained from arms trade statistics compiled by the U.S. Departments of Defense and State through 1983, and some of the 1983 figures were only estimates at the time of data collection. Furthermore, with the exception of security assistance figures for the United States, data for all other countries are only approximations and must therefore be regarded with some caution for the following reasons:

First, U.S. military trade statistics for other countries are based on both open and intelligence sources, which, at best, can be only estimates. Second, there is the problem of translating foreign currencies into a common denominator of dollars for purposes of comparison. Not only do foreign currencies fluctuate on a yearly basis, but so does the inflation factor. Unfortunately, the statistics used here are current dollars and therefore do not account for inflation. Third, these problems are compounded by difficulties involved in estimating the cost of Soviet-produced items – difficulties somewhat mitigated in this study because most of the hardware transferred to the LDCs has been in the export market long enough for trade prices to have been established. According to one source, the accuracy of dollar value figures is correlated with the age and breadth of the distribution of Soviet military equipment.

Costing is least reliable for weapons newly in production and not yet exported. As items are transferred and information about the sales becomes known, earlier estimates are revised to reflect the actual selling price. Over the years, government agencies constantly revise the dollar values as more precise information is received, so that the data for the older items most commonly exported to the LDCs are more accurate than those for newer systems.[8] Nevertheless, these weaknesses in the data need to be kept in mind when assessing the dollar value of non-U.S. military aid programs.

Finally, because available data include only bilateral government agreements, the dollar value of military aid delivered to subnational groups could not be obtained and, therefore, is not included in the statistical tables presented below. For this reason, the discussion on military assistance to insurgents is based on information derived from the general literature and on interviews with government officials.

These then are some of the drawbacks associated with arms export estimates. In the social sciences, however, data sources are rarely, if ever perfect, and so, despite their weaknesses, what statistics do exist are used here to supplement other descriptive materials in an effort to comprehend and compare the dynamics of military assistance during periods of war and peace.

2

Bilateral Military Assistance: The Role of the Superpowers

**Prewar and Wartime Patterns
of Weapons Procurement and Supply:
A Comparison**

Since the end of World War II, bilateral agreements between governments have been the most common means of procuring arms and services for industrializing countries, and most have relied on one principal donor for them.[1] The superpowers have dominated this market. Between 1964 and 1973, for example, the United States and the Soviet Union delivered 81 percent of the military equipment exported to the Third World. Although their combined share dropped markedly in the next decade to 60 percent, and smaller states have increased their arms exports, the United States and the USSR remain the largest single suppliers of military assistance to the LDCs, and they continue to dominate the world's arms trade.[2]

These general trends are reflected in the prewar procurement patterns of the LDC combatants analyzed here as well. Based on the dollar value of military goods and services transferred to them, out of the 14 states involved in the eight wars, nine, or 64 percent, obtained their arms during prewar periods from one major supplier[3]; of these, seven (50 percent) were largely dependent upon the Soviet Union or the United States for military equipment.[4] (See appendix 1.)

During periods of armed conflict the picture changes dramatically, even though the proportion of countries dependent upon the superpowers for military assistance remains constant. Of the 9 countries fighting wars long enough to receive significant resupplies, 5 (56 percent) have relied primarily upon the United States or the USSR for support. This statistic, however, conceals the sharp decline in the total dollar value of superpower aid during wars and the differential effect various types of conflict have upon the procurement behavior of combatants.

As a rule, long wars have had a disruptive impact upon prewar bilateral supplier-recipient relationships.[5] Here change is the norm rather than the exception. For example, of the four LDCs that have waged conventional battles lasting two years or more, all have altered their pattern of procurement because of superpower resupply restrictions. Somalia, which received its military assistance from the Soviet Union prior to the war in the Horn of Africa, turned to Western suppliers and established a diversified pattern of procurement after its onset. Ethiopia, on the other hand, which previously received matériel from a variety of Western states, became almost totally dependent upon the Soviet Union during and after the war. Iraq, principally reliant upon the Soviet Union before it invaded Iran, remained dependent but also further diversified its suppliers, purchasing more equipment from the West, East Europeans, and other Third World countries as the war progressed. Iran, originally a dedicated U.S. customer for military hardware and services (75 percent of its total procurement), was forced to purchase arms wherever they were available, even across blocs. Thus, although three of the four states engaged in long conventional wars had relied mainly upon one of the superpowers for military assistance before hostilities began, only two continued to do so during wartime, and only one, Iraq, maintained a (reduced) supply relationship with its original donor (see tables 3 and 4). For all four, even Ethiopia, the dollar value of military assistance from diversified sources rose dramatically. (See appendix 1.)

TABLE 3

Patterns of Procurement and Supply During Conventional Long Wars: A Comparison of Prewar and War Periods[1]

Prewar		War	
Monopoly/ Principal (M/P)[2]	Diversified/ Multiple (D/M)[3]	Monopoly/ Principal (M/P)	Diversified/ Multiple (D/M)
Conventional Wars			
Somalia[4] (USSR)	Ethiopia[5]	Ethiopia[4] (USSR)	Somalia[5]
Iran[5] (U.S.)			Iran[6]
Iraq[4] (USSR)			Iraq[6]
Insurgencies			
Honduras[5] (Israel)	El Salvador[5] (U.S./Israel)	Honduras[5] (U.S.)	
Afghanistan[4] (USSR)	Nicaragua[5]	El Salvador[5] (U.S.)	
	Morocco[5]	Nicaragua[4] (USSR)	
		Afghanistan[4] (USSR)	
		Morocco[5]	

1. Derived from appendix 1.

2. M/P – one supplier provides 50 percent or more of all military assistance to a recipient.

3. D/M – two suppliers each contribute 45 percent or more; or three or more suppliers, none of which provide more than 49 percent of a recipient's military assistance.

4. Eastern Bloc

5. Western Bloc

6. Mixed, Cross-Bloc

TABLE 4
Patterns of Procurement in Long Conventional and
Insurgent Wars: A Comparison Between Prewar
and Wartime Periods[1]

	Change		No Change	
Type of War	*M/P to D/M[3]*	*D/M to M/P*	*M/P*	*D/M*
Conventional[2]	Somalia Iran Iraq	Ethiopia		
Insurgencies		Nicaragua El Salvador Morocco	Afghanistan Honduras[4]	

1. Derived from appendix 1.

2. Short-war combatants – Syria, Israel, Argentina, the PRC, and Vietnam – are not included.

3. M/P – Monopolistic or Principal supplier (one supplier provides 50 percent or more of all military assistance to a recipient). D/M – Diversified or Multiple suppliers (two suppliers each contribute 45 percent or more; three or more suppliers, none of which provide more than 49 percent of a recipient's military assistance).

4. Honduras changed from Israel (prior to 1979) to the United States as its principal supplier.

The pattern for insurgencies has been somewhat different. While fighting insurgencies, governments have not changed bloc suppliers, and whereas most governments fighting long conventional wars have received less direct assistance from the superpowers, those involved in insurgencies have grown more dependent upon them.[6]

Central America serves as an example. As violence has increased, the size of U.S. military assistance programs to El Salvador and Honduras has risen. By 1983, El Salvador was receiving 80 percent of its military aid from the United

States in contrast to 51 percent during the prewar period when Israel was another major source of supply (46 percent). And U.S. deliveries of equipment and training to Honduras have been growing. Nicaragua, once dependent upon a variety of sources, was reliant upon the Soviet Union for 56 percent of its military assistance by 1983.[7] Since 1982, a similar pattern has developed in Morocco, which then began receiving a larger proportion of its aid from the United States. Even the government of Afghanistan, almost totally dependent upon the Soviet Union for its training and equipment before the coup against Prime Minister Mohammad Daud in 1978, has received almost five times as much assistance since then.

Overall, levels of aid have risen dramatically during recent wars, and they have stimulated increased transfers from diversified sources as well (see table 5 and appendix 1).[8] This is true for unconventional as well as conventional conflicts. Among governments facing insurgencies, aid from Western Europe rose 23 percent; from Eastern Europe almost 90 percent; and from the Third World more than 450 percent.

Although the number of combatants principally dependent upon the superpowers for military assistance remained about constant and the dependency of those fighting unconventional wars upon them deepened, the dollar value of U.S. and Soviet aid fell precipitously from a prewar yearly average of $6 billion to $2 billion. As a proportion of total aid to the combatants, their share declined from its prewar level of 75 percent to 38 percent. The U.S. contribution alone dropped from an annual prewar average of $2.5 billion to $156 million or 2.7 percent of total wartime assistance to combatants. Deliveries from other sources have expanded proportionately, with Third World suppliers showing the largest gain, growing from not quite 3 percent before war to 22 percent of total military assistance during periods of combat.

Short wars, like long unconventional conflicts, have not negatively affected prewar procurement relationships. Those five LDCs involved in hostilities that only lasted from a few

TABLE 5

Dollar Value (millions averaged) and Percentage Change of Military Assistance to Combatants During Prewar, War, and Postwar Periods[1]

Combatants	Prewar	War	% Change	Post-war	% Change Prewar
Ethiopia	46.4	765.7	+1550.0	286.0	+516.4
Somalia	80.6	152.8	+89.6	105.7	+31.1
Afghanistan	28.3	132.5	+368.2	−	−
Morocco	207.2	358.8	+73.2	−	−
Nicaragua	8.5	46.4	+446.0	−	−
Honduras	15.5	7.7	−50.3	−	−
El Salvador	3.5	30.1	+760.0	−	−
Vietnam	40.5	−	−	691.4	+1607.2
PRC	112.5	−	−	121.5	+8.0
Iran	2029.9	784.2	−61.4	−	−
Iraq	1849.6	3291.8	+78.0	−	−
Argentina	373.6	100.2	−73.2	831.6	+122.6
Syria[2]	2203.2	−	−	1521.2	−31.0
Israel	885.0	−	−	790.4	−10.7

1. Derived from appendix 1.

2. Total Soviet resupply to Syria in 1983 not included. Dollar values for Soviet resupply of Syria in 1983 are only conservative "best" estimates based on mid-1983 figures.

weeks to a few months (Syria, Israel, Argentina, Vietnam, and the PRC) have all maintained their original prewar supply patterns. Israel and Syria continue to receive most of their equipment and services from the United States and the USSR, respectively. Argentina has not changed its practice of obtaining weapons from a variety of largely Western sources, except, of course, Great Britain. Vietnam has remained dependent upon the Soviet Union for military assistance, and China continues to purchase defense technologies sparingly and selectively from a number of Western countries. One obvious reason for this continuity is the time factor. Finding alternate sources of compatible matériel and arranging for significant deliveries quickly has been impracticable and sometimes unnecessary given the short duration of hostilities. Therefore unlike long wars, short wars have had only marginal impact upon established military assistance ties, but even among these combatants, a rise in the number of suppliers and the dollar value of their deliveries is evident in the postwar period.

For most warring states, then, periods of armed conflict have forced changes in their style of procurement. Some have changed bloc orientation, some have become more dependent upon a principal supplier, while others have turned to diversified sources for their defense needs. In quantitative terms, while the dollar value of military aid to most combatants has escalated during conflict, the contribution of the superpowers, particularly the United States, has declined, and other suppliers have moved in to meet the demand.

Differences between Eastern and Western Styles of Military Assistance

Size, Speed, and Quality of U.S. and Soviet Arms Deliveries

Eastern and Western bloc military assistance programs generally differ in both content and pace of delivery. The Soviets, for example, have tended to follow a "surge pattern," delivering large amounts of equipment relatively quickly. The U.S. Central Intelligence Agency (CIA) estimates the average time lapse between contract and delivery of Soviet arms to be one-half to one-third that of the United States.[9] This delivery style stands in marked contrast to the West's, which is characterized by smaller numbers delivered over a longer period of time. In part, this is attributable to the Soviet production style.[10] In contrast to the United States, the Soviet Union, which in any case produces large numbers of weapons for its own forces, further adjusts its production schedules with the export market in mind, permitting fast delivery of great quantities, particularly during wartime emergencies.[11] The development of the Soviet IL-76 long-range cargo plane and the expansion of the Soviet maritime fleet has improved the Soviets capability in this regard.

According to some sources, however, the airlift capability of the Soviet Union should not be exaggerated or compared to that of the United States. The Soviet Union has experienced difficulty in developing a high by-pass engine that is capable of hauling heavy weights over long distances. For example, the Il-76 (similar to the U.S. C-141 in weight), which was developed in the mid-1960s, has a small capacity in comparison to other U.S. cargo aircraft. In addition, it is fuel inefficient and does not have an in-air refueling capability. The Il-76 therefore has relatively "short legs" and can cover only limited distances without landing for refueling – something that involves obtaining permission from sometimes unsympathetic governments for landing rights. The same is true for the Soviet's larger AN-22 transport, which has also suffered recurrent engine problems and crashes. The AN-400, the first Soviet transport to use a high by-pass engine – sometimes referred to as the "C-5sky" in U.S. military circles – began production in 1986 and so did not play a role in recent wars.

One U.S. State Department official claims that contrary to popular reports, the Soviet's have never conducted a massive airlift to a client. Ninety-five percent of all Soviet military deliveries have been made by sea. Even the Ethiopian airlift, often cited as an example of Soviet airlift capabilities, delivered at most 10 percent of the Soviet equipment transferred to the Mengistu regime, with most arriving by sea.[12] The psychological effect, however, of delivering even small amounts of heavy equipment by air to clients engaged in battle has been great – perhaps greater than its military importance.

The Soviet's newest cargo vessels have considerably increased their sea delivery capabilities, however. Oversized equipment can now be rolled on and off these ships without the need for assembly and so can be delivered more quickly and efficiently. In this area, the Soviet's capability is significantly greater than that of the United States. Overall, then, the Soviet Union, like the United States, has the capacity to deliver large amounts of heavy military items more quickly than any other state in the international system, although the Soviet Union is more likely than the United States to resort to this style of bulk resupply to clients during wartime.

An analysis of the dollar value of transfers to the combatants and their inventories during prewar, war, and postwar periods illustrates the differences. Note in table 5 that, with one exception, the largest proportional increases in the dollar value of military assistance during wartime occur among Communist-supplied recipients (Ethiopia – 1,550 percent; Nicaragua – 446 percent; Afghanistan – 368 percent).[13] A similar resupply effort was launched for Vietnam after its border war with China (1,607 percent). Among the Western-supplied recipients, only El Salvador has experienced a comparable rate of growth (760 percent) over prewar levels.

An analysis of the combatants' force structures presents a similar picture.[14] For example, Ethiopia's prewar arsenal, composed principally of U.S. and Western equipment, was relatively small. Compared with Somalia's, which was Soviet supplied, Ethiopia maintained about one-half the number of combat aircraft (36); one-third the number of tanks (78); and about the same number – one squadron – of helicopters. After Somalia's invasion of the Ogaden in February 1977, the Soviets initiated a military assistance program for Ethiopia unique in the region. In all it amounted to more than $1 billion, three times what the United States supplied Ethiopia during the previous 25 years.[15] In less than a year the Soviets supplied via an air and sealift operation 50 MiG-21 and 20 MiG-23 fighter aircraft and hundreds of tanks and armored personnel carriers. By 1978–1979, the number of planes in Ethiopia's inventory had risen to 99 (a 175 percent increase), and 56 helicopters and 554 tanks were operational (a rise of

250 percent and more than 600 percent respectively). (See appendix 2.) In dollar value, the increase amounted to a 1,550 percent rise in military assistance over prewar levels.

The resupply of Vietnam further demonstrates the Soviet style and capability. Because the PRC/Vietnam engagement was so short there was little time or need – nor, apparently, was the USSR inclined – to send significant assistance. Later in the year, after armed hostilities had ended, a tremendous resupply effort began, providing Vietnam with both more of what it already had in inventory and new items. Phase one emphasized replacement equipment that could be absorbed and maintained immediately, such as tanks (which more than doubled in one year), MiG-21s, and artillery. During phase two, beginning at the end of 1979 and continuing into early 1980, new and more sophisticated deliveries began to arrive: strike aircraft, ground attack helicopters (Mi-24), SA-9 air defense missiles, and the beginnings of a modern navy. (In 1982, 8 Shershen fast attack craft (FAC), 3 Polnochny landing ships for tanks (LSTs), and 14 KA-25 antisubmarine warfare helicopters were newly delivered.)[16] By 1983, the dollar value of Vietnamese arms imports had risen 17-fold or 1,607 percent.

The Syrian resupply effort by the Soviets provides another example. It has been described by Ambassador Robert G. Neumann as "the largest reequipment effort in their history."[17] Various press reports have estimated the cost of resupply (some of it airlifted) to be between $2.5 and more than $5 billion by the end of 1983. The Soviets sent armored personnel carriers (APCs), trucks, T-72 tanks, more than 100 fighters armed with new air-to-air missiles, and ZSU mobile antiaircraft guns and introduced SA-5 and SA-9 surface-to-air missiles into the country.[18] Echoing its massive response to Ethiopia in 1978 and Vietnam in 1979, the Soviet Union reinforced its image as a reliable supplier able to move large masses of equipment rapidly.

These huge increases in military transfers need to be kept in comparative perspective, however. As table 5 demonstrates, although the yearly average of $766 million in aid to Ethiopia represents a 1,550 percent increase over prewar assistance levels, a slightly larger procurement ($784 million, yearly average) constitutes a decline of 61 percent for Iran. Thus in absolute terms the levels of military assistance vary considerably from one combatant to another, determined by the recipients ability to pay, the existing regional balance, and the strategic importance of the area to its suppliers.

Regardless of supplier, the largest resupply assistance has gone to the combatants in the Middle East (averaging between not quite $1 billion and $3 billion per year), followed by countries in Asia and Africa, which have all received less than $1 billion annually (from $100 million to $700 million, averaged), and Central American countries, which have received between 1 and 5 percent of the latter amount (ranging from $8 to $46 million). Although relative to U.S. programs, Soviet equipment has arrived in larger numbers and more quickly, the quantity of matériel delivered by both superpowers to the Middle East cannot be equated with their resupply efforts in other less developed regions of the world.

Qualitative differences characterize superpower styles of military assistance as well. The experience of Western-supplied states, for example, has differed from their Communist bloc counterparts in two major ways. First, their inventories tend to grow more slowly, reflecting in part traditional U.S. ambivalence toward arms transfers as a foreign policy tool, Europe's limited production and delivery capabilities, and Western tactical and strategic orientations toward war. Second, Western-supplied inventories are generally both smaller and more advanced than those supplied by Warsaw Pact countries.

In an effort to assess the relative sophistication of equipment in the LDC combatants' inventories, I used age as an indicator (taking as the base year the item's original production date and subtracting it from the inventory year). This method was based on the assumption that new generations of weapons incorporated modern innovations and are therefore more technologically advanced than older systems. This, of course, is not always the case, particularly for degraded export models or upgraded older technologies. I have tried to account for these variations wherever possible, however.[19]

Appendix 2 and table 6 present the comparative age of items in the combatants' inventories. They illustrate the qualitative differences between Eastern and Western military assistance programs, which are most pronounced in combat aircraft deliveries. A comparison of Ethiopia and Somalia, table 7, shows that in 1976–1977 Ethiopia's Western-supplied inventory was smaller and more modern across the board than Somalia's. By 1979–1980, Ethiopia's switch to Communist sources of supply was reflected in its comparatively larger and older force structure. Somalia, on the other hand, deprived of Soviet military assistance since the beginning of the war, was now dependent upon Western donors. Although the size of its inventory diminished considerably due to general attrition and battle losses, the weapons Somalia did manage to acquire, particularly combat aircraft, were relatively modern, reducing the average age of Somalia's combat aircraft inventory by 5.4 years during the same time period. In general, the supply patterns in recent wars suggest that the displacement of Eastern suppliers by Western donors increases inventory modernity and vice versa.

Here again, we find that major regional differences exist. In the Middle East, intense competition between the Eastern and Western blocs has produced comparatively larger inventories as well as relatively more modern equipment on both sides. Combat planes and helicopters number in the hundreds in Iraq, Iran, Syria, and Israel; tanks and armored vehicles in the thousands. The average age of the equipment is about 17 years. In contrast, Central American inventories are smaller and older. During the early 1980s, in each weapon system category the number of items in inventory remained below 30 and the average age was more than 20 years. The inventories of combatants in other regions range somewhere in between in size and modernity.

*Training and Support As a Component
of Eastern and Western Military Assistance*

Numbers of weapons and other services tell only part of the
military assistance story. Training—the instruction of foreign
personnel in military-related skills, often overlooked by analysts of the arms trade—is a vital component of military assistance programs. Without it, weapons have little utility for
the soldiers who use them; indeed training, or lack of it, has
often determined the outcome in war.

For suppliers, training foreign soldiers has held the promise of important political gains. When successful, it transmits
to the recipient military the supplier's particular orientation
toward war, the doctrine and tactics for which the weapons
were designed, and sometimes a specific world view. Furthermore, through training, especially of foreign officers, suppliers hope to gain political and military allies, and, if they
are fortunate, see some of those they have schooled rise to
a position of power and influence.[20]

Despite the political and military significance of training, it has received little research attention, and accurate
comparative information about military education programs
worldwide is the most elusive of all arms transfer data. (In
fact, given the military importance of and difficulties in gathering intelligence in this area, accurate information probably
does not exist.) Training data, especially information about
the number of personnel trained in countries other than the
United States or the Warsaw Pact, is unreliable (and there
is some question about the reliability of the Warsaw Pact
figures as well). Furthermore, the dollar value of training provided in all countries other than the United States is unavailable. What is presented here, then, is "soft" data culled from
U.S. government sources and anecdotal material gathered
from interviews, the press, and other secondary sources.

As in the arms trade, the superpowers are the largest
suppliers of military-related education and services. There
are major differences in the proportion of training, services,

TABLE 6
Comparative Qualitative Force Structure: Average Age of Weapon Systems in Inventory by Type of System[1]

Ethiopia/Somalia

	1976–1977		1977–1978		1978–1979		1979–1980	
	Ethiopia	*Somalia*	*Ethiopia*	*Somalia*	*Ethiopia*	*Somalia*	*Ethiopia*	*Somalia*
Combat aircraft	15.8	24.8	16.8	25.3	19.2	25.5	20.2	19.4
Helicopters	13.8	20.0	18.1	21.0	19.0	22.9	18.2	23.0
Tanks	23.2	34.4	20.2	32.6	24.7	32.1	25.8	32.1
Armored Personnel Carriers (APCs)	13.0	27.6	17.6	35.4	21.9	25.6	22.3	25.6
Missiles	—	—	—	18.5	8.0	12.8	20.0	15.0

Iran/Iraq

	1979–1980		1980–1981		1981–1982		1982–1983	
	Iran	*Iraq*	*Iran*	*Iraq*	*Iran*	*Iraq*	*Iran*	*Iraq*
Combat Aircraft	7.9	16.0	7.9	13.2	7.9	15.4	7.1	16.1
Helicopters	10.2	16.8	10.8	16.6	12.9	17.1	12.9	15.6
Tanks	17.1	24.7	17.1	23.5	13.7	24.7	16.9	25.6
APCs	22.6	21.7	23.6	22.7	24.7	11.9	25.7	12.9
Missiles	11.0	13.2	12.0	14.2	13.0	15.2	14.0	13.8

Vietnam/PRC

	1978–1979		1979–1980		1980–1981	
	Vietnam	*PRC*	*Vietnam*	*PRC*	*Vietnam*	*PRC*
Combat Aircraft	19.7	24.1	22.3	25.0	16.3	25.8
Helicopters	20.4	20.4	18.2	21.5	18.9	21.7
Tanks	32.0	25.0	25.9	26.0	28.1	29.0
APCs	24.0	12.0	20.3	12.0	21.6	22.0
Missiles	13.2	15.5	14.0	15.5	15.0	15.7

Morocco

	1978–1979	1979–1980	1980–1981	1981–1982
	Morocco	*Morocco*	*Morocco*	*Morocco*
Combat Aircraft	16.6	15.2	15.1	16.6
Helicopters	9.9	11.1	12.5	3.8
Tanks	26.3	21.9	28.0	29.0
APCs	17.0	16.5	14.0	15.8
Missiles	7.2	8.2	9.2	10.2

Afghanistan

	Afghanistan	Afghanistan	Afghanistan
Combat Aircraft	22.1	24.0	26.3
Helicopters	20.9	17.5	17.7
Tanks	26.0	27.3	27.9
APCs	23.5	24.5	25.5
Missiles	8.0	9.0	10.0

Israel/Syria²

	Israel	Syria	Israel	Syria	Israel	Syria
Combat Aircraft	8.2	14.3	10.9	17.1	13.3	15.3
Helicopters	15.5	14.8	15.5	15.1	14.6	15.1
Tanks	27.2	26.7	28.4	23.5	26.8	23.7
APCs	28.1	23.6	30.7	24.6	29.8	25.6
Missiles	7.9	15.3	11.3	16.9	11.9	16.3

Argentina

	Argentina	Argentina	Argentina
Combat Aircraft	13.7	15.3	13.6
Helicopters	15.1	15.2	16.2
Tanks	31.4	23.2	20.5
APCs	19.5	20.4	19.5
Missiles	13.9	16.3	16.1

El Salvador/Nicaragua

	El Salvador	Nicaragua	El Salvador	Nicaragua	El Salvador	Nicaragua	El Salvador	Nicaragua
Combat Aircraft	27.8	19.0	27.3	20.0	27.7	23.0	24.6	24.5
Helicopters	12.6	23.2	13.6	15.7	19.9	16.8	21.1	17.0
Tanks	26.0	37.0	27.0	38.0	28.0	32.5	29.0	31.0
APCs	13.1	—	14.1	—	13.6	—	14.6	—
Missiles	—	—	—	—	—	—	—	—

Source: Derived from *The Military Balance 1976/77–1983/84* (London: IISS, 1976–1983).

1. Average age of each weapon system type in inventory=

$$\frac{\left(\left[\begin{array}{c}\text{Year in}\\\text{LCD}\\\text{inventory}\end{array}\right]-\left[\begin{array}{c}\text{Year of}\\\text{original}\\\text{production}\end{array}\right]\times\left[\begin{array}{c}\text{no. in}\\\text{LDC}\\\text{inventory}\end{array}\right]\right)+\left(\left[\begin{array}{c}\text{Year in}\\\text{LDC}\\\text{inventory}\end{array}\right]-\left[\begin{array}{c}\text{Year of}\\\text{original}\\\text{production}\end{array}\right]\times\left[\begin{array}{c}\text{no. in}\\\text{LDC}\\\text{inventory}\end{array}\right]\right)+\cdots}{\text{Total no. ot weapon system type in inventory}}$$

2. Israel upgrades its old infantry equipment, therefore the date of original production may be unrelated to an item's capability.

TABLE 7
Size and Age of Ethiopia's and
Somalia's Inventories: A Comparison
Between Western and Eastern Supply Patterns[1]

	Ethiopia[2] 1976–1977 (Compared With Somalia)		Ethiopia[3] 1979–1980 (Compared With Somalia)	
	Size	Age	Size	Age
Combat Aircraft	−30.0	+9.0	+78.0	−0.8
Helicopters	00.0	+6.2	+38.0	+4.8
Tanks	−172.0	+11.2	+600.0	+6.3
APCs	−220.0	+14.6	+432.0	?

Source: Derived from appendix 2 and figure 6.

1. Average age of each weapon system type in inventory=

$$\frac{\left(\begin{bmatrix} \text{Year in} \\ \text{LCD} \\ \text{inventory} \end{bmatrix} - \begin{array}{c} \text{Year of} \\ \text{original} \\ \text{production} \end{array}\right] \times \begin{array}{c} \text{no. in} \\ \text{LDC} \\ \text{inventory} \end{array}\right) + \left(\begin{bmatrix} \text{Year in} \\ \text{LDC} \\ \text{inventory} \end{bmatrix} - \begin{array}{c} \text{Year of} \\ \text{original} \\ \text{production} \end{array}\right] \times \begin{array}{c} \text{no. in} \\ \text{LDC} \\ \text{inventory} \end{array}\right) + \ldots}{\text{Total no. of weapon system type in inventory}}$$

2. Western Supplied.

3. Eastern bloc Supplied.

and hardware each has delivered to LDCs, however. On average, weapons and ammunition make up only 38 percent of U.S. military assistance programs, with support equipment, spare parts and modifications, and support services (training, construction, repairs, etc.) constituting the remaining 62 percent. Soviet deliveries are inversely structured (two-thirds equipment; one-third support, spares, and services).[21] It is estimated that in recent years U.S. deliveries of military services have been four times those of the USSR.[22]

In addition, Soviet training programs are not rated as highly as U.S. programs by recipients. Apparently this inadequate training was a major complaint of the Syrians after the 1982 Lebanon war. The large numbers of Soviet advisers sent to help train the Syrian military on the new air defense system since then is thought to be, at least in part, a response to that charge.[23]

Listed in table 8 is the training component of U.S. military assistance programs to LDCs engaged in recent wars. It gives some idea of the relative proportion of training services to other types of U.S. military-related transfers. Although the percentage varies considerably from one country to another, and in some instances is very small, the U.S. military education program is still the largest in the world when compared with other suppliers. Between 1955 and 1981, counting only military personnel from combatant states, the United States has trained nine times more men than have the Warsaw Pact countries.[24]

The Central American states have received proportionately more training aid (grant-aid) than states in other regions. As table 9 indicates, military education programs in Central America are not just a function of the present regional conflict, but characterize U.S. military assistance programs to these countries since 1955. Although the number of El Salvador's military trainees grew sharply in 1982 and 1983 and a similar rise is occurring for Honduras, the transfer of hardware and other services has also increased so that the proportion of training to other military assistance in real terms has declined. In general, however, training is a politically less sensitive issue than weapon transfers and is therefore more likely to be funded by the U.S. Congress.

Most military-related instruction is provided by the superpowers directly to LDC recipients, but during conflicts both have enlisted the aid of allies and friends. In each of the wars examined here, other countries have supplemented the training efforts of the United States or the USSR, and in politically delicate situations in which one of the superpowers has chosen to keep its distance, they have served as indirect sources for this form of aid. (See discussion below.)

Unfortunately, information on the number of foreign military personnel given what type of special military educa-

TABLE 8
Military Training as a Percentage of
Total Military Assistance Provided by the
United States to the Combatants[1]
(Dollar Value, 1950–1982)

Afghanistan	100.0%
Argentina	7.0%
China	0.0%
El Salvador	17.8%
Ethiopia	9.4% (1953–1977)[2]
Honduras	57.8%
Iran	4.6% (1950–1979)
Iraq	2.5% (1955–1971)
Israel	0.5%[3]
Morocco	3.7%
Nicaragua	64.7%
Somalia	3.3%
Syria	98.2%
Vietnam	?[4]

Source: Department of Defense Security Assistance Agency (DSAA), *Fiscal Year Series As of September 30, 1984* (Washington, D.C.: Data Management Division, Comptroller, DSAA, 1984). Data on the dollar value of Foreign Military Sales Program (FMS) training provided by DSAA, June 1985.

1. International Military Education Training Program (IMET), a grant-aid program and training procured under the FMS. Included are training programs offered at U.S. facilities. The figures do not include military advisory or technical teams in the field.

2. U.S. military assistance began in 1953 and ended with the onset of the Horn war.

3. FMS only, no IMET.

4. Training figures not disaggregated for Vietnam. Included with equipment in the Military Assistance Security Fund (MASF), a special fund set up by the Department of Defense during the Vietnam War.

tion by the United States and USSR is unavailable. Nevertheless, it can be assumed that if the superpowers have been reluctant to transfer their most advanced systems to the LDCs in general and to the combatants in particular, then the associated advanced technical training transferred also has been minimal.

As the above statistics suggest, there are important differences in the amount of support services provided by the two superpowers as well. Traditionally, U.S. military assistance agreements have contained provisions for large numbers of extra parts and components as well as sufficient support equipment and maintenance training. Soviet programs have been quite dissimilar.

Although the Soviets have increased their training services over the years, their policy with regard to the transfer of spare parts and maintenance facilities has been fairly constant. Because the Soviet Union is a continental power, they have traditionally supplied their own forces from secure areas in the rear. They have followed a similar pattern in supporting clients, which in practice, if not in intent, has afforded the USSR some measure of leverage over them. As a rule, the USSR has been careful not to provide its customers with large numbers of spare parts or significant maintenance and repair capabilities. Soviet hardware transfers to noncombatants are characterized by small numbers of spares, and unlike the United States, most agreements do not contain a spare parts resupply clause. Resupply is, therefore, almost always a favor to the recipient and at the Soviet Union's discretion. This approach in part determines the size of their aid package to combatants and explains why, when the Soviets decide to resupply, their deliveries are so large.

For similar reasons, relatively few recipients of Soviet military assistance are permitted overhaul or depot repair facilities. Major repairs on major systems must be done in the Soviet Union.[25] In Afghanistan, for example, the long war has demonstrated both the character and weaknesses of the Soviet Union's 34-year-old prewar military assistance program. During the initial phase of the conflict, troops were

TABLE 9
Training of the LDC Military Personnel in Communist Countries and the United States
Number of Trainees and Percent Increase, 1955–1981

	Soviet Union and Eastern Europe							U.S.							
	1955–1975 Total	1977	1978	1979	1981	1955–1981 Total		1955–1975 Total	1977	1978	1979	1980	1981	1955–1981 Total	
	No.	No.	No.	No.	No.	No.	% <	No.	No.	No.	No.	No.	No.	No.	% <
Ethiopa	–	–	–	–	2,095	2,095	+100.0	3,683	47	–	–	–	–	3,914	+6.3
Somalia	2,450[a]	100[a]	0	0	50	2,600	+6.1	–	–	–	–	–	21	21	+100.0
Morocco	150	0	0	0	0	145[b]	0.0	2,130	85	199	109	129[c]	150[d]	2,934	+37.7
Afghanistan	3,550	475	0	0	1,555	5,580	+57.2	419	14	20	–	–	–	487	+16.2
Iran	275	50	0	0	70	395	+43.6	10,601	–	–	–	–	–	10,601[e]	0.0
Iraq	3,200	875	275	50	10	4,410	+37.8	410	–	–	–	–	–	410	0.0
Syria	3,825	525	600	0	565	5,515	+44.2	20	–	–	–	–	–	20	0.0
Israel	–	–	–	–	–	–	–	–	–	–	–	–	–	–	–
Vietnam	–	–	–	–	–	–	–	47,935	–	–	–	–	–	47,935	0.0
Nicaragua	–	–	–	–	260	260	+100.0	4,976	234	275	6	–	–	5,737	+15.3
Honduras	–	–	–	–	–	–	–	2,619	116	219	226	166	261	3,863	+47.5
El Salvador	–	–	–	–	–	–	–	1,708	47	–	–	125	256[h]	2,369	+38.7

Argentina
Total: — — — — 3,803 140 — — —[g] — 4,802 +7.3

Combatants: 13,450
Total: 21,000 +56.1 78,304 — — 83,093 +6.1

All Third World: 41,200[f]
57,795 +40.3 354,287 — — 380,253 +7.3

Source: For Soviet Union and Eastern Europe, 1955–1975, 1977, 1978, and 1979: CIA, Handbook of Economic Statistics, 1976; 1978; 1979; 1980 (Washington, D.C.: GPO); and for 1981 and 1955–1981, U.S. Department of State, Soviet and East European Aid to the Third World, 1981, Publication 9345 (Washington, D.C.: Bureau of Intelligence and Research, February 1983). For the United States: U.S. Department of Defense Security Assistance Agency, Fiscal Year Series, as of September 1982. Includes IMET (grant-aid training) program only. FMS and commercial training not included.

% < = percent increase

a. Does not include 25 trained in China.

b. Unexplained discrepancy; possibly corrected figure.

c. Seven more Moroccans were trained under FMS.

d. Five more Moroccans were trained under FMS.

e. In 1973, Iran stopped receiving IMET, paying for its own training through FMS. In 1979, there were 760 Iranians training under FMS. After 1979, all training programs ended.

f. Total for 1955–1975 does not include 3,000 trained in China. The number of LDC military personnel actually in training in 1975 was 3,775, not including 625 trained in China.

g. Sixteen Argentine military personnel were trained under FMS.

h. In 1982, the number rose to 747 military personnel trained by the United States.

housed and field maintenance performed in hastily construct-
ed tents outside cities or next to airfields. Since then, some
new in-country repair and maintenance facilities have been
established (particularly for vehicles), but Soviet aircraft still
must be ferried to depots inside the Soviet Union for overhaul
and major repairs. "If it can't be fixed in 10 to 30 minutes,
leave it," is still the rule.[26]

Clearly, this policy places a heavy support burden on the
Soviet Union in wartime situations. Apparently, however,
from the Soviet perspective, the potential control these restrictions afford is worth the price of arranging large-scale
maintenance and resupply to clients during wartime.

In general, then, differences between the superpowers'
arms transfer policies are reflected in their training and service programs as well. Countries principally supplied by the
Soviet Union tend to have larger inventories (with fewer
spares and maintenance equipment) and receive less training,
whereas the recipients of Western military assistance have
smaller inventories and receive more military-related training
and support assistance.

Impact on Recent Wars

There is some evidence to suggest that these variations in
style of military aid have had important consequences for the
LDC combatants. For example, during recent conflicts, large
prewar inventories appear to have been more destabilizing
than smaller, more modern ones. In all of the conventional
wars surveyed here, countries with numerical superiority
were the aggressors, such as Somalia, the PRC, Argentina,
and Iraq. In the latter case, Iraq had agreed reluctantly to
a diplomatic resolution of the Shatt al Arab dispute in 1975
when Iran had the military advantage, but invaded Iran in
1980 after Iran's arsenal had diminished through attrition
and its armed forces were weakened through revolutionary
disarray. Somalia, with three times the number of tanks and
armored vehicles and twice the number of combat aircraft,
attacked Ethiopia in February 1977. The situation in the

Falklands was not very different. Although Argentina's force structure was only about one-third the size of Britain's, given the scanty deployment of British forces in the Falklands and the long logistical pipeline for resupply, the Argentine military calculated on their numerical (and psychological) advantage and acted upon it.[27] And in Asia, the PRC, with four times the number of men and a huge inventory, attacked to teach Vietnam a lesson.

On the other hand, smaller, newer inventories with better trained and motivated soldiers have not served the defenders badly. Iran, despite the disarray of its U.S.-trained and equipped military, turned a rout into a stalemate, and Britain, despite the disadvantage of distance, defeated Argentina in 11 weeks. In Asia, the PRC failed to achieve a decisive military victory. During the recent wars fought in the Third World, although quantitative advantage has encouraged adventurism, the qualitative advantage of the defenders in both men and matériel has decided the conflict's outcome.

Similarities between U.S. and USSR Resupply Patterns: Cautious Restraint and Global Competition

As the discussion above indicates, both superpowers have exhibited distinctive styles of military assistance. During wartime, however, the similarities may outweigh the differences. Public impressions to the contrary, both superpowers have shown concern about escalating Third World conflicts with arms exports and have exercised restraint, particularly during the early stages of the war or until some obvious political or strategic advantage has been perceived. Whatever the gain to be derived from immediate support, the United States and the Soviet Union have weighed it against both the cost of alienating the other combatant and driving it into the arms of the other superpower and against the possibility of initiating a direct U.S.-USSR confrontation in the region. Thus, during recent short wars, the United States and the

USSR refrained from resupply altogether, and in other longer wars have also refused to do so, at least during the initial, confusing stages of the conflict.[28] For example, at the beginning of the Ethiopian-Somalian hostilities, both superpowers temporized. Although many analysts attribute a rapid and generous response on the part of the Soviet Union to the Ethiopian request for aid, in fact, when approached by the Provisional Military Administrative Council, the Dergue, before the war in 1975, the USSR reacted cautiously, "far from convinced . . . that a convergence of interest yet existed between Moscow and the *Dergue*."[29] It was not until October 1977, seven months after the war over the Ogaden began and after the Carter administration had denounced the Mengistu regime on human rights grounds and announced the end of military aid to Ethiopia, that the Soviet Union began to assist the new government. Only at that point did Moscow initiate large-scale emergency deliveries of approximately $1 billion in arms to Ethiopia. In the United States, the long debate and indecision of the Carter administration regarding aid to Somalia continued throughout the war. U.S. military assistance to Somalia did not actually start until after the armed conflict had ended, when small amounts of U.S. training and equipment deliveries began in 1981.[30]

During the initial phase of the Iran-Iraq war, the superpowers were equally cautious. The United States immediately embargoed all military supplies to both sides. For its part, the Soviet Union sharply restricted its arms deliveries to Iraq, while it cautiously flirted with Iran. Fulfilling only prior contracts for small arms and munitions, it refused to provide direct and new military supplies to Iraq. According to a Senate Foreign Relations Committee report, it was not until spring 1982, a year and a half after the war's onset, that the Soviet Union decided to abandon its earlier policy of "neutrality" and support Iraq overtly, calculating that its neutral stance "risked permanently alienating Iraq without compensating gains in Iran."[31]

To date the superpowers continue to exercise moderation in the Gulf war. The United States, since 1982, has only exempted on a case-by-case basis exports of dual-use items to Iraq. And although the Soviet Union has heavily reequipped Iraq with T-72 tanks, new MiG-23s, and SAMs placed around Baghdad and other cities, they have refrained from sending long-range missiles that would enable the Iraqis to disrupt oil tanker traffic at Kharg Island seriously or to "change the strategic balance in the region – meaning that Iraq has received no long-range missiles that could reach Israel."[32]

In addition to denying immediate support to combatants, both the Soviet Union and the United States generally have refrained from releasing technologies deemed to be regionally destabilizing. The apparently modern systems delivered are often actually degraded export models or remain under superpower control. For example, although the Soviets have transferred large amounts of equipment to Syria, there is little evidence to suggest that the level of sophistication of Syria's inventory has been greatly raised as a result. The general assessment among intelligence analysts is that the Syrians have done little more than recoup their losses and that the Soviets are interested in enhancing defensive not offensive capabilities. Furthermore, as of the spring of 1986, the USSR has retained control over the more advanced systems, such as the C^3I system they are building for the two SA-5 air defense complexes sent to Syria.[33]

In Vietnam, the USSR has been equally careful not to transfer its state-of-the-art equipment. To date the Soviets have allowed the Vietnamese only older technologies such as the SU-22 Fitter fighter bomber, a downgraded version of a more advanced Soviet model; the KA-25 antisubmarine warfare helicopter (in production since 1966); and the MiG-21 (vintage late 1950s or early 1960s).[34] The more modern Soviet equipment now in Vietnam belongs to the USSR and remains under tight Soviet control.[35] Even in Afghanistan, the Soviets appear to have learned from the U.S. experience in Vietnam. According to one analyst, they decided from the beginning to limit their investment and appear to have settled for controlling the principal Afghan towns and highways. The Soviet contribution to the Afghan military averages less than

$200 million a year, and their total investment in the war has remained low.[36] In Central America, Soviet military assistance to Nicaragua is powerful by regional standards, but has been limited in dollar value (on average $26 million yearly) and level of sophistication. In general, the USSR transfers systems that have already been deployed in Soviet units for several years. Even when they are released for export, they are often modified versions that are stripped of their most sophisticated subsystems. Those that are not, as in the case of the Syrians, remain under Soviet control for extended periods of time.[37]

Although U.S. arms transfers to the LDCs have tended to be more modern than the Soviets', the United States also has been reluctant to part with state-of-the-art equipment that might be "destabilizing," particularly to countries in areas of conflict. The inventories of Communist-supplied countries are on average only 8 to 10 years older than those of U.S. recipients. In some regions such as Central America, the force structures of Honduras, El Salvador, and Nicaragua (originally Western equipped) are older than those of some Communist clients in Africa and the Middle East. As one observer of the Central American war complained, "Most of the equipment from the U.S. is used; often it is very old and sometimes it is junk."[38]

In addition to restraint, superpower resupply programs, both during and after recent wars, have been conditioned on significant political or military concessions from the combatants. This has been true for all types of armed hostilities — short wars, insurgencies, and longer conventional conflicts. U.S. arms transfer restrictions in 1982–1983 to induce Israeli compliance in Lebanon and the Soviet resupply of Vietnam in 1979 in exchange for Soviet access to Vietnamese bases are only two examples.[39]

The latter agreement illustrates the strategic advantages that often accompany superpower resupply efforts. Until the arrival of Soviet aid in 1979 there was no evidence that the Vietnamese had allowed a significant Soviet presence inside their territory, nor were there significant arms transfers from the USSR to Vietnam. After the Chinese invasion, however, as a quid pro quo for military and economic assistance, the Vietnamese government gave the Soviets permission to use Cam Ranh Bay and Da Nang bases. As a result, the strategic character of East Asia has been changed. Soviet surface ships and submarines make regular visits at Cam Ranh Bay, allowing them improved, if still limited, naval capabilities in the South China Seas. In addition, the new facilities have helped the Soviets expand their intelligence gathering and communications capabilities in the region.

Syrian-Soviet relations in 1982 provide an interesting third example. In 1977, despite its dependence upon the Soviet Union for military assistance, Syria apparently rejected a Soviet request for military "facilities" or bases.[40] Whether or not this issue was related to the Soviet's delayed response to Syria's pleas for resupply in June 1982 is unknown, but tensions between the two countries rose to new heights at that time. Syria had lost almost 100 planes and virtually all of its antiaircraft defenses. The Soviet decision to comply with Syria's request in late 1982 was probably motivated by a desire to recoup its international reputation as a reliable supplier, but strategic considerations evidently influenced the decision as well. Syria remains the only game in town for the Soviets, and even though no formal base rights have been granted, 5,000–7,000 military advisers and technicians accompanied the resupply package.[41] Moreover, they have obtained limited access to ports and airfields in Syria, and the large Soviet presence has facilitated their intelligence gathering capabilities in the region. From the Soviet perspective, the rewards of resupply were not insignificant.

Political and security considerations have also determined the speed and dedication of the superpowers' commitment to governments fighting insurgent wars. Their concern with avoiding any negative change within their spheres of influence has prompted them to respond more decidedly to countries such as Afghanistan (the USSR) and those in Central America (the United States), then to countries in the "fringe" regions of the world.

The U.S. reaction to a Moroccan request for arms during its struggle with Polisario guerrillas in the Western Sahara is a case in point. As long as U.S. policymakers did not see or agree upon a clear cut strategic or political gain, the United States did not offer significant assistance. Throughout the period of the Carter administration, the pros and cons of the Western Sahara issue were furiously debated, paralyzing the policy-making process and polarizing parts of the government.[42] Only after a constellation of external and domestic forces was in place and the political advantages perceived was a clear military aid policy formulated.[43] Up until that point, Morocco's sources of supply were limited and necessarily diversified.

The Soviets, on the other hand, anticipating few political gains, were not more forthcoming to the opposition. Although Soviet allies reportedly provided some indirect assistance to the Polisario, the USSR did not recognize the insurgents, nor did it break off its trade relations with Morocco.[44]

In 1982, the administration of President Ronald Reagan, concerned about access to the southern Mediterranean and the Persian Gulf after the fall of the shah, saw Morocco, with its strategic location at the mouth of the Strait of Gibraltar and its deep water harbors, as an important strategic asset. It could serve as a convenient staging or refueling post for U.S. forces, provide important communications facilities, and offer alternate transit rights for U.S. aircraft should Spain and Portugal deny them. Thus, in exchange for U.S. access to Moroccan ports, bases, and communications stations, the Reagan administration agreed to lift President Jimmy Carter's restraints on military transfers to Morocco and raised its Foreign Military Sales (FMS) credits from $34 million to $100 million for FY 1983.[45]

On balance, U.S. and Soviet security interests have been well served by their restraints on arms transfers. In return for easing embargoes or restrictions and resuming military assistance, both have realized significant strategic and political gains. From the perspective of the United States and the Soviet Union, constraints on resupply during war, when used adroitly, can have as many (if not more) advantages as bilateral agreements during peacetime.

In short, both superpowers have used military assistance as a foreign policy tool both to further their political interests and to prevent any loss of influence in regions of strategic importance. In an effort to avoid any escalation of local conflicts that might affect them adversely, they have been notably restrained in their resupply efforts. Even in those instances in which political advantage has been sought by keeping the war alive through arms transfers (e.g., the U.S. assistance to the Afghan rebels and the Soviet support of the Sandinistas) the responses of the United States and the Soviet Union have been moderated by their global concerns and responsibilities.

3

Diversification and Indirect Sources of Supply: The Response of the Combatants

Diversified Sources of Military Hardware

In recent years, diverse suppliers of military technology and indirect transfers have become attractive alternatives to sole source arrangements for LDC combatants, especially for those fighting long wars. From their point of view, when one or both superpowers cease direct resupply or make unacceptable political demands, there are few other options.

Constrained by the need to find equipment that can be integrated easily into existing inventories without time-consuming training in maintenance and operations, LDC combatants have increasingly resorted to European or Third World producers as well as to less orthodox means of resupply. Smuggling or illegal transfers, often with the acquiescence of an interested foreign government; third party transfers, whereby equipment sold to one government by another is delivered to a third with or without the permission of the original seller; purchases from the private international arms market; weapons left in battle zones after a conflict — these are only some of the indirect methods of arms acquisition used in recent wars.[1]

In the past, insurgent forces were the primary recipients

of this form of aid, largely from Communist bloc sources. Restricted by embargoes, the need for secrecy, the limited monies they were able to solicit from friendly foreign governments or sympathetic groups, and the logistical problems involved in securing deliveries, guerrillas have continued to rely on one or more unorthodox channels for their arms supplies. In some instances, in addition to circuitous weapons imports, cottage industries produce bombs, explosives, crude rifles, and pistols and perform upgrading tasks. The PLO established several small arms factories in Lebanon, and the Afghan rebels have maintained similar industries for rifles and ammunition in the North West Frontier area.[2] These sources are often supplemented with raids on government stores and with equipment supplied by defecting government troops. In Central America, for example, official U.S. estimates suggest that roughly half of the arms used by Salvadoran guerrillas and 20 percent of their ammunition and explosives are U.S.-supplied items taken from the armed forces of El Salvador.[3]

Recent wars suggest that diversification is now a common procurement style for other types of armies as well. In all conflicts examined here, other than the short PRC-Vietnam border conflagration, there has been a demand from one side or the other, and often both, for diversified and indirect sources of supply. In response, a wide assortment of donors have transferred military equipment to governments as well as insurgents. The West, taking its example from Communist bloc states, has been transferring matériel through a variety of channels. Just as there has been in recent wars a historical reversal of tactical roles with as many insurgencies being fought by anti-Communists against Marxist regimes (e.g., the Contras in Nicaragua and the rebels in Afghanistan) as by leftist insurgents against non-Marxist regimes (e.g., the Polisario and the Sandinistas) — so, too, many different sources, direct and indirect, have supplied both government forces and guerrillas.

A combination of political and economic factors has

helped to reinforce this trend. First, there has been an increase in the number of governments able and willing to export a wide variety of Eastern and Western-derived arms.
A rising number of states produce military equipment, en-
larging further the pool of available suppliers, particularly
for the technologically less advanced implements of war such
as small arms, ammunition, machine guns, light cannons, artillery, patrol boats, and light armor. Even states that do not
manufacture arms have found the means, often clandestine,
for sending equipment from their own inventories to the combatants. In this way, the world's growing arsenals and military production capabilities have served to make multiple
direct, as well as indirect, sources of supply an attractive
alternative for all sides in recent wars.

Second, the East-West ideological orientation of Third
World buyers and their suppliers is in decline. As a result,
combatants have had access to a larger, politically unre-
stricted population of donors. During the Horn war, as noted
above, both Somalia and Ethiopia changed their principal
source of military supply, turning from East to West and vice
versa. After the Somali-Soviet relationship deteriorated, a
mixed bag of suppliers began provisioning Ethiopia – the
Soviet Union, Libya, South Yemen, Vietnam, Cuba, East
Germany, Bulgaria, China, and Israel. This strange ideological conglomeration – Israel aligned with virulently anti-Israe-
li and Communist countries and China allied with the Soviet
Union – did not seem to concern the new "Marxist" Ethiopian
regime, nor, for that matter, its supporters. Similarly, the
Gulf war has seen an eclectic group of suppliers providing
assistance to Iraq and Iran, and sometimes both. Since the
beginning of the war, out of 40 suppliers, 10 – Communist and
non-Communist alike – have delivered military equipment to
both sides. (See table 10.)

Finally, superpower restrictions have made procurement
from diverse sources a necessary method of resupply during
conflict. In some cases, the participants have had no other
choice. In others, they hoped these acquisition methods would
reduce superpower leverage over them.

TABLE 10
Arms Resupply and/or Support to Iran and Iraq, 1980–1983

Country	Iraq	Iran
Algeria		X
Argentina		X
Austria	X[a]	
Belgium	X[b]	
Brazil	X	X[c]
China	X	X
Czechoslovakia	X	
Egypt	X	
Ethiopia	X[b]	
France	X	X[d]
Germany, Democratic Republic of	X	X
Germany, Federal Republic of	X[e]	
Greece		X[b]
Hungary	X	
Israel		X
Italy	X	X
Jordan	X	
Korea, North	X	X
Korea, South		X
Kuwait	X[f]	
Libya		X
Morocco	X[g]	
Pakistan	X	
Philippines	X[f]	
Poland	X	
Portugal	X[b]	
Saudi Arabia	X[f]	
South Africa		X
Soviet Union	X	X[h]
Spain	X	
Sudan	X[i]	

(continued)

TABLE 10
(Continued)

Country	Iraq	Iran
Switzerland	X	X
Syria		X
Taiwan		X
United Arab Emirates	X*f*	
United Kingdom	X*b*	X*b*
United States	X	X*j*
Vietnam		X
Yemen, South		X
Yugoslavia	X	

Source: Derived from *SIPRI Yearbook, 1984* (London: Taylor and Francis, 1984), 198–199.

a. GHN-45 155-mm howitzers via Jordan.

b. Small arms, ammunition, or spares.

c. Armored vehicles via Libya.

d. Last three of 12 Kaman Class FACs ordered 1974.

e. Bo-105 helicopters direct and from Spain; Roland-2 SAMs from Euromissile; tank transporters.

f. Financial support.

g. Other support
h. Via Libya, North Korea, Syria, and Warsaw Treaty Organization countries.

i. Training, military advisers, or troops.

j. Not officially sanctioned; private dealers and individual companies.

In combination, these factors have had an important impact on the arms trade during combat. In each of the seven wars described below, multiple and indirect sources of supply have played a significant role. This pattern is particularly pronounced during long wars, where diversified relationships have become the rule rather than the exception.

The Iran-Iraq War

The sizable attrition rate during this war has produced a frenzied style of arms procurement, often likened to the atmosphere of a Near Eastern bazaar with each side recruiting large numbers of suppliers to satisfy its hardware needs. According to the Stockholm International Peace Research Institute (SIPRI), when the Gulf war broke out, Iraq was receiving arms from three countries (the USSR, France, and North Korea), while Iran was supplied by five (the United States, the USSR, France, Italy, and Britain). Now some 29 countries supply Iraq and 21 supply Iran; of these, 10 support both sides. In addition, both combatants rely heavily on private arms dealers and circuitous delivery routes via third countries for their small arms, munitions, and spare part transfers.[4]

Iraq's response to Soviet supply restrictions before and during the Iran-Iraq war serves as a good example of how one LDC has attempted to use diversification and multiple sources of supply to reduce superpower control. Iraq, since the late 1950s and early 1960s, received the bulk of its equipment from the Soviet Union. But when the Soviets imposed limitations in 1973, Iraq established trading relations with other countries, particularly France, which agreed to provide combat aircraft as part of a comprehensive air defense system.[5]

In 1980, at the beginning of the Iran-Iraq war when the USSR once more applied transfer constraints and halted all but token deliveries of spare parts and replacements for the approximately 80 planes Iraq lost in battle with Iran, Iraq turned again to France for much of its aerospace needs.[6] This decision required Iraq to diversify its sources of training as well. Since then, Iraqi pilots have been trained in France on the Mirage F-1 (in Iraq's inventory since 1981) and in Great Britain on advanced jet trainers.[7] In addition, although the United States has maintained an official hands-off attitude toward the Gulf war since its inception, Iraq began seeking closer military links. In 1982 permission was granted by the

United States for the purchase of transport aircraft, and later a number of civilian helicopters were sold to Baghdad. A second sale of helicopters was approved in 1985.[8]

Finally, Iraq availed itself of products from Third World producers such as Brazil, from which it ordered ground forces equipment, ammunition, spare parts, bombs, and air-to-surface missiles, and from other LDCs able to provide Soviet equipment, servicing, and spares.[9] China, reportedly in exchange for oil, has supplied tanks, armored personnel carriers, artillery, light arms, ammunition, and replacement parts, and Chinese technicians are assembling Soviet-designed MiG-21s (F-7s) and MiG-19s (F-6s) for the Iraqi air force in Jordan, which maintains a staging base for the assembly and shipment of Chinese fighters to Iraq.[10] Both Egypt and Jordan have supplied technical support to assist in maintaining the aircraft.[11] Moreover, Egypt has been an indirect conduit for retransfers from several different producer-suppliers. During 1982 alone, arms exports to Iraq originating in Egypt were estimated at close to $1 billion.[12]

According to SIPRI, the Federal Republic of Germany, Italy, Spain, Czechoslovakia, the German Democratic Republic, Hungary, Poland, Yugoslavia, Austria, Switzerland, and North Korea have also directly transferred major military items to Iraq. Some, along with Belgium, Portugal, the United Kingdom, Pakistan, Morocco, Ethiopia, and the Sudan, have provided small arms, munitions, training, and spares as well. Although the Soviet Union eventually resumed deliveries of aircraft and armor, Iraq, mindful of past experience, has continued its pattern of diversified procurements and according to one observer "clearly prefers Western-made equipment."[13] Although the USSR is still Iraq's main supplier, France has moved to second place.

Iran, on the other hand, confronted with the continuing U.S. embargo, has had no option other than indirect sources for its military supplies. Libya and North Korea have been the two governments willing to negotiate direct bilateral arms agreements with Iran. As a result, Iran's air force, with planes mainly of U.S. manufacture, has deteriorated to the point at which it can no longer defend its own airspace.[14] It has been forced to rely on cannibalization of its own stocks, the open market in Europe, and Israel for spare parts. During the first two years of the war, Israel provided about $300 thousand worth of spare tires for Iran's F-4 fighters and other spare parts.[15] Israeli technicans were also reported to be helping Iran keep some of its F-14s operational.[16] Israeli assistance stopped some time in 1983, however, and since then the Iranian air force has had to depend on less direct sources. There have been unsubstantiated but persistent rumors that Iran, in desperation, has negotiated to buy MiG-19s (F-6s) from China or North Korea.[17]

Training has proved to be another problem. Dependent principally upon the United States for military equipment prior to the revolution, Iran had sent large numbers of military personnel to the United States for instruction. Between 1955 and 1973 alone, 10,601 were trained in U.S. facilities. After the revolution, as the supply of major U.S. systems dwindled, so too did U.S. training programs. Rumors have continued to appear in the press about Chinese F-6 aircraft arriving in Iran via indirect routes, along with talk of an aircraft conversion training program for 200 mujaheddin under way in East Germany, but by spring 1986 Iran had not received any new fighter aircraft nor had any large-scale foreign training programs associated with them taken place.[18]

Iran's major supplier of ground equipment has been North Korea. According to several reports, the North Koreans and Iranians have had a countertrade arrangement, oil for arms, since early in the war. The agreement is said to stipulate the exchange of 250 thousand tons of crude oil in return for about $1 billion worth of military equipment. By mid-1983, Pyongyang had supplied about 30 percent of Iran's arms needs. By mid-1984, some observers believed the proportion had risen to 40 percent.[19] These deliveries are believed to have included large quantities of ammunition, 12,000 machine guns and rifles, 1,000 mortars, 600 antiaircraft batteries, some 400 artillery pieces, and 150 Soviet T-62 tanks.[20] Although some of the items were domestically produced, apparently most were of Chinese and Soviet origin. In addition, some U.S. parts from Vietnam, F-5 spares, and cannibalized parts were transferred as well.[21]

Syria and Libya also have been important conduits of Soviet weapons. Over the war years they have reportedly delivered Katyusha rocket artillery, surface-to-air missiles, antiaircraft guns, APCs, small arms, and antitank missiles. And both have served as purchasing agents for Iran – Syria in Western Europe and the Soviet bloc countries and Libya in Italy and Spain.[22]

Until late 1983 or sometime in 1984, other suppliers such as Israel, South Africa, and South Korea provided some spare parts for Iran's U.S.-origin ground systems, ammunition, small arms, and some quartermaster supplies, and Brazil and China sent a variety of matériel as well – all but Israel, using an intricate maze of third parties and indirect routes to do so.[23] These deliveries provide an interesting picture of how the subterranean arms bazaar operates. Soon after the war began, items such as Cascavel EE-9 armored vehicles, grenades, rockets, ammunition, and bombs made in Brazil but purchased earlier by Libya for its own inventory arrived in Iran via Syrian cargo planes.[24] Apparently, Iran approached Brazil directly in 1983, but in response to various international pressures Brazil demurred, publicly announcing its policy not to sell to both sides in a conflict. As a Brazilian industry representative declared: "Brazil does not want, under any circumstances, to jeopardize its relations with Iraq, its main supplier of oil and a regular buyer of equipment and special services in general."[25] Since then, a triangular trading operation reportedly has been added to the indirect Libyan route, with trading companies in Portugal and Spain purchasing matériel and reselling it to Iran.[26]

China's equipment, on the other hand, reportedly has been sent to Iran via North Korea and Singapore, although the Chinese government has denied allowing any deliveries at all.[27] In addition, Iranian representatives have been busily buying what U.S. equipment they can from a wide assortment of different suppliers in the gray and black market using other similar indirect methods of delivery.[28]

In general, Iran has been dependent upon a host of third country transfers from other LDCs and the private international arms market for its military supplies. According to one possibly apocryphal story, Iran's dependence on indirect transfers is so complete that private dealers have purchased captured Iranian equipment from Iraq, such as M-47 tanks, howitzers, and mortars, and then resold it to Iran.[29] In fact, no modern major system has been transferred to Iran from any quarter since the onset of the war, a singular success for the worldwide embargo efforts![30]

As in most of the wars analyzed here, arms transfer restrictions have played an important part in determining the course of battle. In no other conflict is this better illustrated than the Gulf war. By July 1984, military analysts were observing that Iran's defense planners had put off a threatened major offensive against Iraq because of concern over whether Iran could provide enough air and tank support for its ground troops.[31] Iran's most serious weakness is in artillery shells, armor, and aircraft. As a U.S. Senate Foreign Relations Committee study reported, the military balance had shifted in favor of Iraq because of "the worldwide arms embargo" of Iran fostered by the United States and because of the large Soviet and French arms sales to Iraq. According to the Senate study, "several key Iranian leaders appear to be reaching the conclusion that the costs of continuing military efforts are becoming too great."[32] But whether this is true or not, superpower restraints have obviously dictated the indirect pattern of Iran's arms supplies and stimulated Iraq's diversified acquisitions.

The Falklands War

During the Falklands war, Argentina's attempt to acquire arms through traditional bilateral government channels were also thwarted by a Great Power embargo.[33] Only Israel and a few of Argentina's traditional allies in Latin America were forthcoming with spares, technical assistance, and supplements for the French and U.S. equipment already in Argentina's inventory. Venezuela provided spare parts for the

Mirages as well as aviation fuel, and Peru transferred a small number of French Mirages. Brazil sold two EMB-11 Bandeirante reconnaissance aircraft and ammunition, and there is some possibility that Brazil also sent Argentina a larger package including patrol aircraft, air-to-air missiles, and anti-aircraft ammunition.

Israel's deliveries were larger and more varied than the others and provided a major source of equipment to Argentina. They are said to have included Gabriel air-to-ship missiles and Shafrir air-to-air missiles and spare parts for other U.S. weapon systems in Argentina's inventory.[34] Shortly after the war, Israel also sent a number of Dagger (Nesher) fighters – the Israeli version of the French Mirage III, accompanied by technical advisers to assemble them.[35] Libya is also thought to have delivered some compatible French items.[36]

Argentina chose not to request significant assistance from the Soviet Union, and the Soviets in their turn cautiously offered, and may have supplied, limited intelligence support.[37] Since the end of the war, in the face of continuing U.S. restrictions on arms sales to Argentina (only defensive equipment has been authorized), Argentina has remained reliant on France and other, mostly Third World, suppliers for its aerospace needs.

As in the case of the Iran-Iraq war, restricted transfers played a significant role in the Falklands conflict. Because of the embargo imposed by the European Common Market, the French refused to fill Argentina's orders for additional Exocet missiles. For the Argentines this meant that once the five missiles in their inventory were expended, they were compelled to rely on unguided bombs, most of which did not detonate. "Releasing the bombs at very low altitudes (less than 40 feet) at which the Argentine pilots were forced to fly, did not give the bombs sufficient time to arm themselves prior to impact."[38] Although arms transfer restrictions were not solely responsible for the limited capability of Argentina's air force, they contributed to it. Had Argentine aircraft been able to inflict greater damage on the British fleet, the outcome of the conflict might have been very different.

The Horn War

Before Somalia entered the Ogaden in February 1977, it had
established a secure military relationship with the Soviet
Union. By that time, in exchange for access to bases at Ber-
bera and Mogadishu, the Soviets had delivered $400 million
worth of equipment to Somalia, supplemented by $20 million
worth of assistance from other non-Communist states. But
in August 1977, the Soviets branded Somalia's act an aggression and stopped all military assistance to them. The United
States followed suit shortly thereafter, also refusing military
support to the Somalis. As the war progressed, a curious
alignment of direct and indirect suppliers appeared. In response to massive Soviet deliveries to Ethiopia and Somalia's
declining fortunes in the war, the Arab states, with some
small arms assistance from Iran, organized a large military
effort to help Somalia. It was reported that Somalia was
buying equipment for its Soviet inventory from Egypt, which
was paid for by Saudi Arabia.[39]

Israel, finding itself in strange company, nevertheless
continued to provide military assistance after Ethiopia changed
its bloc orientation.[40] It sent some equipment, helped train
Ethiopian troops in its use, and performed maintenance on
Ethiopia's U.S.-origin, F-5 fighter planes, while Soviet and
Cuban military personnel assisted the beleaguered Ethiopians in the field and trained them in new Soviet technologies. East German technicians were also alleged to be supporting the Ethiopian military, and other Eastern bloc allies
and friends such as South Yemen, Vietnam, Bulgaria, and
Libya were providing additional forms of military aid.[41]

Central America

The unpopularity of the anti-insurgency war in Central America within the U.S. Congress and among the press and the
Reagan administration's concern about possible imposed limitations on U.S. involvement again opened the door to indirect sources of military supply to the combatants. Israel, for

example, now supplements U.S. assistance in the region, which marks a departure from its previous activities in Central America as an independent supplier of arms. In the opinion of one journalist, the new role has brought "Israel closer to acting as a surrogate for the United States."[42] Israel is now, as in the past, one of the main suppliers of weapons and expertise to Guatemala, Honduras, El Salvador, and more recently the Nicaraguan rebels (the Contras). According to the press, at the request of the United States Israel has sold weapons captured from the PLO to Honduras for use by the Contras as well as some Western-origin systems and has provided indirect financial assistance.[43] In addition, Israel reportedly is involved in military training in the region and is consulting with Costa Rica and Guatemala about intelligence operations.[44]

Along with Israel, Honduras, El Salvador, and Argentina, even private U.S. organizations are providing indirect assistance to the Nicaraguan guerrillas, reportedly "replacing the United States as a key source of aid."[45] From 1982–1984, Argentina alone reportedly sold at least $10 million worth of arms to Honduras for shipment to the Contras, in addition to $9 million in quartermaster and other sales to El Salvador. In 1984, in spite of a change of regime stemming from the disastrous Falklands war, Argentina sent $2.5 million in arms to the Contras. And the Brazilians, regardless of their declared policy of noninvolvement in the Central American conflict, secretly sold eight counterinsurgency versions of the Tucano T-27 to Honduras in a package that includes support materials, training, and technical support. Some reports maintain the planes are likely to be used for operations near the Nicaraguan border.[46]

Multiple suppliers have given military assistance to Nicaragua's Sandinista government too. Cuba, the USSR, Eastern Europe, members of the PLO, and Libyan personnel have all participated. Equipment from the Soviet Union (estimated at $130 million between 1979 and 1983) has been supplemented by indirect transfers of Soviet systems from Libya to the Sandinistas, according to one report.[47] On both sides, then, different kinds of assistance from many quarters, direct and indirect, have arrived, enabling the combatants to continue their armed struggle.

The War over the Western Sahara

The Polisario guerrillas, active in the Western Sahara since the departure of Spain in November 1975, have from the beginning supported their military efforts from indirect sources. Initially, Land Rovers and light arms stolen or captured from withdrawing Spanish units were supplemented with miscellaneous shipments of small arms. Later, as the intensity of the war increased and the Polisario force declined in number, mercenaries were recruited from several black and Arab states – Libya, Algeria, South Yemen, Nigeria, Mali, Guinea, Upper Volta, and Chad, among others – and Libya and Algeria began providing important matériel aid. According to Moroccan intelligence reports, by mid-1985 the Polisario had accumulated 120 Soviet-made T-55 tanks and BMP APCs, 60 Katyusha rocket launchers, 9 122-mm artillery pieces, and 9 160-mm mortars – all supplied by Algeria.[48] Other sources, however, credit earlier Libyan deliveries with at least some of the T-55 tanks, as well as SA-6s and Brazilian Cascavels.[49]

Like its enemy, the Moroccan government has also benefited from indirect and diverse sources of support. During the early years of restricted military assistance and funding from the United States, with France providing only limited relief, King Hassan turned to third parties such as Egypt and South Africa for supplementary military assistance and to Saudi Arabia to help pay for arms purchases.[50] By the 1980s, U.S. and French assistance rose, and other European states began sending military items as well. Spain, for example, reportedly sold arms to Morocco, along with the United Kingdom, West Germany, Italy, Romania, Poland, and others.[51]

War in Afghanistan

Twelve days after Soviet troops crossed the Afghanistan border, the CIA had outlined its plans for indirect arms transfers to the rebels. For the most part, the United States sought either Soviet-made small arms and ammunition or replicas to make them untraceable to their real suppliers.[52]

By mid-1981, the CIA was coordinating a complex, far-flung program involving five indirect sources of aid and between $20–$50 million per year in equipment and training for the Afghans.[53] Each of the various donors has played a distinct role. The United States provides financial assistance, arranges the purchase of some weapons on the international arms market, and is the operation's primary planner and coordinator. Saudi Arabia has undertaken the other major financing role, while Egypt offers training for the guerrillas and serves as a major supplier of arms in addition to China. Both countries have retransferred weapons originally obtained from the Soviet Union along with large amounts of replicated Soviet armaments produced in their own factories. Pakistan, in part in exchange for a $3.2 billion U.S. aid package, has permitted the weapons to move across its 1,400-mile border with Afghanistan and has tolerated training camps within its territory.[54]

In addition to these sources of military assistance, Afghan guerrillas have been collecting much of what they need directly from Soviet arsenals and from disenchanted or greedy Soviet and government troops. According to one source, "Soviet soldiers are the best source of reliable, inexpensive weapons for the resistance movement, and the AK-47 assault rifle is readily available on the black market in Afghanistan. Ammunition is commonly bought from Soviet soldiers by children recruited from Mujaheedin families."[55] One account maintains that defecting Afghan army officers provide not only weapons but also training to the guerrillas in the use of captured Soviet equipment and invaluable intelligence.[56] Since December 1980, through this network of multiple direct and indirect suppliers, the Afghan resistance has managed to frustrate Soviet tactics in Afghanistan.

Lebanon

The prewar military buildup of the PLO in Lebanon and the size and diversity of the arms caches captured by the Israelis have been widely publicized. They offer a unique view of the workings and capabilities of a usually hidden network of the arms trade. As of September 25, 1982, some of the equipment captured by the Israelis included

290	Soviet tanks
216	armored vehicles
215	artillery pieces
10,000	tons of artillery shells
40,000	mortar rounds
5,700	Katyusha rockets
11,619	mines
18,950	hand grenades
6,000	tons of small ammunition
24,000	rifles.[57]

And as one Pentagon official observed in reference to the small arms and ammunition the PLO had stockpiled in hiding places throughout Lebanon, " . . . the Israelis probably didn't find half of it."[58]

Most of the captured PLO arms, transferred by sea and air via Syria and acquired from a variety of illegal, secret, and third party channels such as Hungary, Syria, South Yemen, Saudi Arabia, and Libya among others, were produced in the Soviet Union and other Communist countries, with a sprinkling of West German and U.S. arms represented.[59] Financing came from Saudi Arabia, Kuwait, and Libya and is estimated to have totaled $400 million a year, or approximately $1 million per day.[60] In all, about 12 countries are believed to have offered training and matériel assistance to the PLO. Moreover, large numbers of recruits from Pakistan, India, and Bangladesh served in the ranks of the PLO, augmenting their number.[61]

Diversified Sources of Training

Weapons, as many combatants sadly discovered, are relatively useless without training in doctrine and their operation and maintenance. Therefore, when a combatant finds its established method of weapons supply has been disrupted, it must seek new channels for training as well as hardware. Although weapons may be available from third countries or another willing major supplier, unless the equipment is similar to that already in inventory, conversion training is necessary. Note the change in training patterns for Ethiopia, Somalia, Iran, Iraq, and Nicaragua presented in table 9, page 28. All have changed arms suppliers and have had to seek instruction from sources familiar with their new weapons.

Although there is no empirical data available, recent experience suggests that during long armed conflicts, multiple sources are apt to share in military training efforts whether the combatants have changed principal suppliers or not. This holds for all three types of training situations discussed below, training abroad, on-site training, and training in contiguous areas.[62] When armed hostilities have continued, new weapons have been acquired at various phases of the conflict and different kinds of military instruction have then become necessary. As a result, the combatants have sought and received training assistance, which more often than not has involved many suppliers. At times this diversified training pattern has reflected a principal supplier's way of sharing the support burden; at other times, it has been the only avenue open to embargoed forces.

Training Abroad

Governments facing armed attack as a rule initially receive "emergency" training from in-country advisers. Because equipment that requires extensive training can be assimilated only slowly into inventory, the fighting forces examined here, constrained by the need to conduct an on-going war, have concentrated first on obtaining compatible small arms and munitions along with field training in new tactics and small arms techniques.

Learning how to operate and phase in major systems from new suppliers is a slower, more gradual process. Normally, as a war continues and the operational and maintenance expertise of the recipient increases, training is conducted on a more advanced level, often involving instruction in the supplier country. The latter has often occurred years later and sometimes after combat has ceased. During the Horn war (February 1977 to March 1979), for example, when Ethiopia changed principal suppliers, the training programs with their former Western donors were terminated as well. Only after the war did the Ethiopians begin training in the facilities of their new Communist donors. Table 9 shows that in 1981, 2,095 Ethiopians arrived in Eastern bloc countries four years after the onset of the Horn war and the beginning of Soviet military deliveries, and more than two years after hostilities had officially ended.

But because training abroad during combat takes place only when wars last long enough to make it possible, this form of military education more often than not has involved combatants fighting unconventional wars. For example, Salvadoran army officers apparently have received instruction in Israel, and pilots and crews from Nicaragua have traveled to Bulgaria and other Warsaw Pact countries for advanced military education.[63]

Insurgents, by the nature of their tactics and organization, have relied even more heavily than government forces on this form of support at a wide variety of locations. Palestinians, for example, in addition to training in the Soviet Union and other Warsaw Pact countries, have been taught special skills in North Korea and in a number of other Communist and non-Communist countries.[64] Yugoslavia has provided courses for staff officers in commando and chemical warfare. Vietnam has trained pilots and antiaircraft gunners. Pakistan has given advanced instruction to military engineers, gunboat captains, pilots, antiaircraft battery commanders, and communications officers. India has prepared Palestinians to be military engineers and armored company commanders, and China has supplied instruction for engineers as well.[65]

Libya, too, identified as a principal location for training and advising insurgent and terrorist movements, has been an important instructional source for the Palestinians. A series of training camps in Libya are reported to have provided military instruction and assistance to such diverse groups as the Irish Republican Army (IRA) and the Basque Euzkadi Ta Askatasune (ETA), along with the Palestinians and insurgents from other Middle Eastern and African areas.[66]

Cuba is also said to be a main training center for insurgents, particularly those from Central and South America. Although the Cuban government has denied it, the U.S. press has reported an active "training base for revolutionaries" operating on the Isla de la Juventud, where Nicaraguans and Angolans are receiving various kinds of military instruction.[67] Groups from other Central and South American countries are said to have received training in other parts of Cuba as well.

The West has sponsored similar activities. Small groups of Nicaraguan Contras have been trained under the guidance of Cuban exiles in the southern Californian desert as well as near Miami, Florida and other unspecified locations – with the knowledge of the U.S. government.[68] And Egypt has trained Afghan rebels at Egyptian bases, arming them prior to their return to Afghanistan.[69]

On-site Training

Information about on-site training during combat is scarce and probably even less reliable than that available about instruction abroad. In spite of incomplete data, however, what does exist indicates that both the West and the East have over the years substantially increased their on-site efforts in the Third World. In FY 1960, 78 percent of all U.S. military advisers served in LDCs. In FY 1968, this proportion increased to 94 percent, apparently stabilizing at approximately that level.[70] In 1975 there were 8,090 Soviet and East European military technicians stationed in the Third World, whereas in 1981 there were a total of 18,205, a rise of 125 percent.[71]

Many other suppliers have also provided this kind of support service. More than other forms of military assistance, on-site training has involved a particularly large number of sources. In each of the wars examined here, a wide variety of foreign training teams have carried out in-country advisory tasks for at least one of the combatants before, during, and/or after the armed conflict. Even in Afghanistan, East Germans and Cubans have assisted the Soviets with their military education effort.[72] Ironically, as observed above, a supplementary source of Afghan rebel training on Soviet equipment comes from defecting Afghan government soldiers. In effect, the Soviets and their allies inadvertently are teaching the martial arts to both sides.

During other wars the number and variety of foreign advisers has been larger. In the Horn, Soviets, East Germans, Cubans, and Israelis have helped prepare the Ethiopian military during and after its war with Somalia.[73] Along with basic training on new technologies, the Israelis have instructed counterinsurgency teams and performed maintenance on Ethiopia's U.S.-origin F-5 fighter planes.[74]

In Vietnam, after the incursion of Chinese troops, Warsaw Pact advisers increased in number. By 1983, there were about 2,000 Soviet advisers in-country who were helping the Vietnamese assemble new Soviet equipment, giving technical guidance in its operation, training pilots, repairing and servicing weapons, and maintaining and operating radar facilities.[75] They have been assisted by an unspecified number of East Europeans and Cubans.[76] In Iran, at least one contingent of North Korean instructors has arrived along with North Korean ground equipment deliveries.[77] And during the Sahara War, the PLO was reported to be training Polisario demolition and sabotage experts.[78]

A similar situation exists on both sides in Central America. In Nicaragua, reportedly 1,500 to 3,000 Cuban "military and security" advisers, 50 Soviets, and 35 East Europeans (primarily East Germans, but including some Bulgarians, Czechoslovakians, Poles, and Hungarians), and 50 Libyan and PLO advisers were in-country in 1983 instructing the Nicaraguan armed forces in a variety of operational and maintenance functions. According to one U.S. government report, about half the Soviet advisers and most of the East Germans have provided assistance to Nicaragua's internal security organization. The Libyans have been servicing the Nicaraguan's Polish-built Mi-2 helicopters, and about 30 members of the PLO have been providing pilot training and aircraft maintenance. These specialists have been augmented by hundreds of economic advisers.[79]

Western countries have also provided on-site training in the region. Israelis, for example, have been engaged in several advisory missions there and have assisted U.S. military trainers in El Salvador.[80] Unverified reports that the Angolan rebel group, the National Union for the Total Independence of Angola (UNITA), at one point sent advisers to assist the Contra insurgents have also been received.[81]

In the Middle East, the Soviets have supplemented arms deliveries with large scale technical assistance programs to Syria accompanied by large numbers of Soviet technicians and advisers.[82] Assisting them are said to be more than 300 North Korean advisers. Thus in-country military instruction has been provided by a wide variety of suppliers—governmental, insurgent groups, and, as in the case of Afghanistan, by defecting members of the enemy's force. This type of training is apparently one of the most ubiquitous forms of military aid to Third World combatants and one that is in greatest demand.

Training in Contiguous Areas

Information on advisory efforts in areas contiguous to combat areas is equally fragmented, but, clearly, these activities have also increased in recent years and have played an important role in recent wars. Insurgencies, particularly, have prompted this type of "indirect" assistance.[83]

In Latin America, as noted above, Cuba operates training camps for groups from El Salvador, Nicaragua, Guatemala, Costa Rica, Honduras, and other Central and South American countries.[84]

In the Western camp, the United States and Argentina also offer military instruction within the region. Argentina has trained Salvadoran military officers, and the U.S. Army School of the Americas in the old Panama Canal Zone is now playing an important role in reshaping U.S.-supported forces in Central America. The army school has graduated more than 42 thousand Latin American soldiers during the last 37 years, and enrollment is reported to have risen from a low of 700 in 1980 to approximately 2,400 students in 1983. Of these, almost half are reported to be Salvadorans.[85]

In addition, the United States is training Salvadoran soldiers in Puerto Rico and Honduras. A decision was made in 1983 to send 100 U.S. military advisers to Puerto Rico and to triple their number in Honduras (raising the total to approximately 200) to expand training facilities for officers and enlisted men from El Salvador. In Honduras, of the 200 U.S. military advisers stationed there about one-half are helping the Honduran army. The other half are teaching at a new Honduran regional training center, where Salvadoran and Honduran soldiers receive instruction.[86] Other Western advisers are reputed to be coaching the Contras at facilities in Honduras, El Salvador, and Guatemala.

In South Asia, Pakistan provides a training center for Afghan rebels, one that is staffed by instructors from several different countries.[87] And in the Middle East, Egyptian pilots have been training their Iraqi counterparts.[88]

Based on the patterns established in recent wars, it appears that providers of military training are now as diverse and numerous as donors of weapons, if not more so. As sources of weapons have multiplied, so too have the suppliers and locations of training. Although in sheer numbers of LDC personnel trained the Soviet Union and the United States remain the largest purveyors of military instruction, during wartime many other sources have supplemented their services, establishing a diversified pattern of supply for the combatant countries.

Implications for U.S. and Soviet Interests

As the above examples demonstrate, resupply and training from varied, often indirect, donors has become the dominant mode of military assistance during conflict. To many recipients, multiple suppliers have provided not only alternate acquisition opportunities, but the hope of reducing superpower leverage over them.

From the perspective of the United States and the USSR, however, diversification of supply and training to the combatants has not been without its political and strategic advantages. Both perceive that the stakes of war have grown dangerously high, and neither wants to become involved in a regional conflict that may lead to a wider, more destructive superpower confrontation. Consequently, in regional conflicts, the availability of friends and allies eager to sell compatible matériel and training to the combatants and the increasing number of states with indigenous production capabilities have often provided the superpowers with the means to conduct their global competition less visibly. Each has reason to permit, and in some cases promote, alternate sources of supply to armed forces during combat. Indirect transfers no longer provision only guerrilla forces because both East and West now use them to resupply all sides in conventional and unconventional wars. The volume of Soviet and U.S. complaints and "leaks" about the other's covert activities suggest the appeal of this mode of transfer on the supply as well as the demand side of the arms trade.

The implications of diversification for the present and future structure of the arms trade are discussed in chapter 6. Suffice it to say, at this point, that the increased number of suppliers providing equipment and services during recent wars does not appear to have always worked to the detriment of superpower interests and may at times have worked to their advantage.

4

The Role of Indigenous Defense Industries and the Conduct of War: Internal Transfers

The previous chapters have described the kinds of military assistance delivered to Third World combatants by foreign suppliers. This section will analyze the extent to which those LDCs with significant domestic defense production capabilities have utilized their own resources and to what effect.

Logically, one might conclude that internal transfers constitute an important military advantage for Third World countries at war. First, indigenous production capabilities suggest less dependence upon foreign sources for resupply and a way of avoiding political pressure from one or the other superpower during wartime. Second, they imply a capability to provide significant supplies to a country's war effort, particularly in modern, high-attrition battlefield situations. But recent wars do not support this conclusion.

Production of Major Weapons

The sample of countries for this analysis is unfortunately rather small. Among the combatants, only Argentina, China, and Israel produce major weapon systems domestically, and only two of them have demonstrated significant production capabilities – China in quantity and Israel in quality. Argentina's military industries remain largely assembly operations. But given the spread and variety of their industrial skill levels, these countries represent potentially interesting test cases of the differential impact various manufacturing capabilities have on the process and outcome of war. Contrary to expectation, in all three cases, regardless of technological sophistication, indigenously produced military equipment does not appear to have tipped the balance in favor of the producer.

Argentina

Argentina's defense industries turn out a wide assortment of primarily licensed items, most of them only assembled in Argentina. Included are the IA-58 Pucara (a twin turbo prop, ground attack trainer), armored vehicles (VCI-ICV and the TAM tank), a corvette, 155-mm artillery, and a variety of small arms, mortars, ammunition, and missiles.

Despite these capabilities, Argentina's indigenously produced systems took little part in the war over the Falklands. According to Argentine accounts, six sorties were flown from mainland bases by Pucaras in antihelicopter patrols.[1] Other Pucaras, based at Goose Green and Stanley airfields, proved no match for the British Harriers and remained inactive after the first days of the ground war, and no British casualties were attributed to them.[2] Five had been shot down in combat, nine or more were destroyed on the ground, and the rest captured intact on the airfields after the Argentine surrender.[3] Of the sixty Pucaras in service with the Argentine Air Force, twenty-five – the entire complement stationed on the Falklands – were reported lost.[4]

During the ground war, the role of Argentine indigenous weapons in defense of the Falklands was also minimal. Although some indigenous armored vehicles were fielded by the Argentines, because of their weight they bogged down in the muddy Falklands terrain and took no part in the fighting.[5] In all, Argentina lost about 120 planes and helicopters, a cruiser, a submarine, and the entire weapons and equipment of three army brigades, costing a minimum of $800 million.[6]

It was the imported technologies that provided the Argentine military with the few successes they did achieve. Five French Super Etendards and the Exocets fired from them sank two British ships, and the Argentine ground forces claim their Swiss Oerlikon radar-guided antiaircraft guns and the Franco-German Roland ground-to-air missile constituted their most effective defense against air attack.

In spite of its indigenous production capabilities, Argentina found that fighting a long-range war, even against an overextended enemy, required more sophisticated equipment than their factories could provide. Since the end of the Falklands war, Argentina has been rapidly replacing its losses, investing in new weaponry available in countries with more advanced industries.[7]

China

The lessons learned by China from its engagement with Vietnam were no less sobering. In fact an argument can be made that China's reliance on its own defense industries served to constrain rather than enhance its war-fighting capabilities.

By any standard, the PRC-Vietnam confrontation in 1979 was a limited war. China committed no aircraft for combat or troop support, and only light infantry formations, with some supplementary armor, marched across the PRC-Vietnam border to "teach the Vietnamese a lesson." It was a war that the world's largest armed forces supported by the Third World's largest defense industry should have easily won. Vietnam was not only smaller but had no significant defense industry and was completely dependent upon the Soviet Union for its military supplies.[8]

As it turned out, however, the war was not a clear victory for China. First, China did not achieve its primary political purpose—to relieve pressure on Kampuchea by drawing away Vietnamese troops to the Chinese border. Second, although

China succeeded in destroying Vietnamese border installations and capturing five provincial capitals, it did so with great difficulty and high casualties.[9]

Third, the war demonstrated the backwardness of China's aging equipment, for the most part derived from Soviet models of the late 1940s and early 1950s. There is some evidence to suggest that China's limited military commitment was in part due to the military's assessment that its equipment would prove to be inadequate against the more modern inventories of the battle-hardened Vietnamese. As one study concludes,

> The Mig-17s/19s/21s of the PLAAF [People's Liberation Army Air Force] would have been at critical risk in any engagements with the air units of the SRV [Socialist Republic of Vietnam]. The bombing and attack aircraft of the PLAAF, the I1-28s and F-6bis, would have been at similar risk in the air defense environment created by the SAMS and interceptor capabilities of the SRV. Any significant losses in major air combat and ground support craft which might have resulted would have revealed major weaknesses within the PLAAF, so the Chinese Communist military command apparently opted not to disclose these deficiencies.[10]

For the Chinese leadership, the war highlighted, among other things, the drawbacks of outmoded equipment, antiquated doctrine, and indigenous production without foreign technical assistance or procurement. Yang Dezhi, the deputy commander on the Vietnam front, is quoted as saying:

> This battle has brought up a number of new questions for our military, political, and logistical work, and also provided us with new experiences. All of these will have a profound influence on the revolutionization and modernization of the army.[11]

Today, China's leadership is faced with a dilemma: balancing their need for military modernization against their fear of economic and political dependency. Thus far the government has moved slowly, procuring dual-use technologies such as transport helicopters and computer and civilian aircraft designs, engines, and plant equipment – items that will help modernize both civilian and military industries.[12] They are also upgrading existing platforms with new weapons and components, reportedly with some Israeli technical assistance.[13] There is some skepticism among analysts, however, about whether China can effect military modernization during a time of financial stringency and political uncertainty. One analyst predicted that it might be the late 1980s or beyond before mid-1970s technology could be absorbed. "The qualitative gaps between indigenous output and the state-of-the-art will remain at least ten years."[14]

Israel[15]

The lessons learned from Israel's experience are more difficult to assess. Unlike Argentina and China, Israel fought three kinds of war in Lebanon – a tank war, attacks on the Syrian SAM missiles, and air-to-air battles. Because of the number of different systems involved and the reticence of the Israelis regarding their strategy and tactics, reliable information about which systems were used for what purpose and how they performed is not readily available, and there, has been much controversy among analysts on this question.

Since the end of the Lebanon war in 1982, Israel's indigenous arms capabilities have engendered excited attention from the press. Various sources believe Israel's homemade weapons were a major factor in Israel's fast victory over Syria.[16] One commentator claims that some of Israel's equipment was superior to anything yet deployed by either the North Atlantic Treaty Organization (NATO) or the Warsaw Pact.[17] Others believe it was U.S. technology that won the war. They point out that U.S. equipment heavily outweighed Israeli products in inventory then and that Israel continues to be heavily dependent upon the United States for many systems, not to mention the financing of its military and industrial programs.[18]

On the ground, attention focused on the Israeli Merkava tank (powered by a U.S. engine). Its basic design, innovative armor, and the ammunition for its 105-mm gun were thought to have played a special role in the war. But despite reports about the Merkava's excellent performance in the field, relatively few were actually available for battle. Israeli production of Merkavas is still relatively slow. Only some 200 Merkavas had been produced by the beginning of the 1982 war, a small fraction of the nation's some 3,000 main battle tanks (MBTs) in inventory and only 16 percent of the 1,240 tanks (mostly upgraded, rearmored British Centurions and U.S. M-60s) that bore the brunt of the battle in Lebanon.[19]

Battle reports concerning Israel's antitank tactics centered not only on tank-to-tank combat, but also on the use of helicopters, remotely piloted vehicles (RPVs), and attack aircraft. Apparently the Israelis employed an adroit mix of U.S. technology with indigenous systems and tactics. A major innovation saw the use of RPVs (the Israeli aircraft industry's "Scout" and Tadiran's "Mastiff"), which could hover over battlefields and transmit photo intelligence by direct data link to command centers and perhaps to helicopters hovering behind nearby ridge lines. Some observers noted the technology itself was not new, however. Although the United States had not deployed battlefield RPVs, U.S. prototypes existed, which one source claims the Israelis adopted and modified.[20]

But whether of truly indigenous design or not, it was clear that the RPVs included important components from the United States and were supported and complemented by many other foreign systems. It was the combination of these systems and the innovative tactics employed that made the difference. The information the RPVs acquired was transmitted to missile-firing U.S. Cobra and Hughes 500 helicopters, giving the Israelis a considerable advantage over the attacking Syrian tanks.[21]

Another account believes the most effective antitank weapon used in Lebanon was the tank, and the most potent tank armament was the U.S. L7A1 105-mm gun, used with Israeli-made ammunition, the M-111 Arrow armor-piercing fin-stabilized discarding sabot (APFSDS) round. It is credited with 60 percent of all the Syrian tanks destroyed.[22]

In another of the combat arenas – the suppression and destruction of Syria's SAMs – Israeli achievements were considered equally remarkable and much credit was given to the venturesome use of the Samson target drone. They were used for "tickling" and confusing the Syrian SAM radars, which could then be targeted and destroyed. Although there was considerable confusion regarding the design origin of the Samson, according to one source it was developed in the United States by Brunswick Corporation, but never built. The Israelis produced the Samson under license in Israel and in 1982, using unique tactics, employed it in Lebanon.[23]

Considerable confusion has also marked reports about the weapons actually used to destroy the Syrian SAM sites. Some refer to the use of an Israeli surface-to-surface missile, the Ze'ev, thought to have been used in conjunction with the drones.[24] Others speculate on the use of long-range field artillery.[25] Most, however, put major stress on air-to-surface radiation missiles combined with well-rehearsed aerial tactics. Some reports claim that Israeli-modified, U.S.-built Shrike and Standard antiradiation missiles (ARMs) were fired from F-4E fighter bombers during these attacks.[26] Again, however, regardless of whether Israeli technologies were or were not employed, the success of the total operation depended upon a combination of systems – many of them foreign – and the imaginative use to which they were put.

In the third arena, the air-to-air combat, which produced the astonishing 86 : 0 kill ratio, U.S. F-15s were used to fly top cover for the F-16s (or F-4s) and Kfirs.[27] Here, too, there were rumors of indigenous air-to-air missiles. One report referred to a new Python system, but others assumed most of the lethal kills were made with U.S. AIM-9Ls and perhaps AIM-7Fs.[28] Clearly, again, whether U.S. technologies alone or in combination with Israeli systems were involved, it was the innovative way in which they were used and the array of supporting equipment – such as battle-management radar and computers aboard E-2Cs linked to ground command centers giving the Israelis real-time knowledge of all Syrian aircraft movement on their runways – that made the difference.

Aside from the three main components of the war – tank vs. tank, aircraft vs. SAMs, and aircraft vs. aircraft – Israel improvised with other indigenous ground and naval equipment. Although U.S. field artillery platforms played a major role in the war, the Israelis added a new artillery C3 system, featuring the David computerized fire direction center manufactured in Israel.[29] New artillery fuses and munitions also appeared.[30] But again, it was Israeli devices in combination with imported systems that performed so well.

Although naval warfare was not a major factor in the 1982 war, the Israeli navy did serve important supportive functions. It conducted amphibious landings allowing Israeli forces to leapfrog and cut off PLO forces along the Lebanese coastal road; later it blockaded and aided the bombardment of West Beirut.[31] Israel's navy, more than its air force or army, is built on Israeli-produced systems, again primarily derivative of foreign design. Its new version of the Gabriel ship-to-ship missile was not, however, tested in this war.[32]

In spite of the publicity regarding Israel's domestic military production capability, there is a consensus among defense analysts that weapons were not crucial to the outcome of the Lebanon war. This conclusion is not meant to denigrate the role played by U.S. and Israeli equipment. Without it the attacks surely would have been less successful and more costly. Israel's systems and creative modifications to foreign technologies filled important gaps in their inventory.[33] But the majority of analysts believe that whether of indigenous manufacture or not, the technologies themselves were less responsible for the Israeli military victory than the qualitative human factors of planning, training, and command.[34] As one U.S. observer pointed out,

> The Israelis developed an integrated, advanced command and control network involving real-time air-to-ground data links which worked. They were the first to make it work as a system. They fought the war of the future. Equipment didn't matter. If you switched the weapons the results would have been much the same![35]

Production of Small Arms, Ammunition, and Spare Parts

In our discussion, thus far, there has been no mention of the role played by small arms, ammunition, and spare parts factories in expanding the war-fighting capabilities of producer countries. Many specialists believe that indigenous production of these items somewhat mitigates the need for resupply during conflict. Because so many countries manufacture this type of equipment, however, and because indirect, discreet means of delivery are readily available, the advantages associated with their indigenous production may be overestimated, particularly for short conflicts. Furthermore, the fact that Israel stockpiles these items, a lesson learned from the 1973 Middle East war, suggests that surge production capabilities, even in Third World countries with relatively sophisticated industries, may be more of a problem than generally acknowledged.[36] The LDCs' production output generally is slower and less efficient than that of the industrialized states, and even the latter depend upon stockpiles to keep forces fighting during the initial stages of a large-scale war. For example, a U.S. Air Force inquiry, published in 1984, revealed that U.S. stockpiles of ammunition, spare parts, and supplies were designed to last for a 90-day period "in which the military supply industry was supposed to bring production to a level where output of such supplies was more than consumption in battle."[37]

For Third World combatants, the ability to produce consumables during peacetime has not translated into an ability to deliver sufficient resupplies to troops during combat, particularly in high attrition battle situations. This has certainly been true for the Israelis who are forced to mobilize a citizen army for war and, in so doing, seriously deplete their industries of the highly skilled technicians needed to sustain normal production rates.

Because the producers examined here all fought short wars, it is difficult to evaluate the role indigenous defense industries might play in longer, low-intensity conflicts. Under those circumstances, domestic production might contribute at least some of the necessary matériel – and make a difference. But indigenous industrial facilities for Argentina, China, and Israel and logistical capabilities for Argentina and China were insufficient to provide their own troops with technologies adequate to cope with short high-attrition combat.

In conclusion, the evidence indicates that the military production efforts of warring states have had limited impact on the outcome of recent wars. In China's case the defense-industrial capabilities of its factories have determined the age and quality of its army's inventory, which has, in turn, generated considerable pessimism among U.S. analysts about China's ability to defend itself.[38] Argentina's industries were unable to prevent or moderate the country's humiliating defeat. And not even Israel's domestically produced equipment has been given credit for Israel's victory.

Thus, in recent wars internal transfers have not provided LDCs with either a military or political advantage. All remain dependent upon outside suppliers for the financial or technical assistance necessary to keep their production lines open and for the advanced weapons that keep their inventories modern. Ultimately, the constraints that limit the war-fighting capabilities and political independence of nonproducing combatants limits producers as well.

5

The Effectiveness of Arms
Transfers During War

This study has examined the type and amount of military assistance given to combatants in the Third World. I have described the varying capabilities of suppliers and have shown how their military assistance programs have changed in size and quality during different phases of the combatants' conflicts. How effective military assistance has been during conflict and whether certain types of aid have been more or less useful are questions I will address in this section.

The Human Factor

The preceding discussion suggested that factors other than hardware determined the outcome of armed conflict for producers of military equipment. The analysis below corroborates this for nonproducers as well. Numbers and quality of arms transferred have proved poor predictors of performance in battle for both producers and nonproducers. Although many factors determine the strategy, tactics, and outcome of war, a major constraint on the efficacy of arms transfers for the combatants examined here has been what is called "the human factor." This term generally refers to any one or all of the following conditions: low troop morale, poor command and control, inadequate logistics, insufficient training in the operation and maintenance of equipment, and a poor grasp of the tactics and strategy of the war for which they were designed.

Often underestimated by suppliers and recipients alike, this element appears to have been crucial to the success or failure of those combatants studied here. On the basis of the evidence presented below, the delivery of new technologies without adequate instruction in and preparation for their use apparently has served to retard rather than advance the ability of LDCs to wage war. Even in the Middle East where LDC inventories are the largest and most modern, human capabilities rather than arms have determined the course of battle.

This is not to say that certain individual services may not have the skill to achieve dramatic results with modern weapons, such as the Argentine air force, but this is unlikely to be true for the military as a whole. As a rule Third World forces do not comprehend the potential of modern weapons, nor do they, as one study concludes, "develop the units and tactics to employ them, or equip themselves with the spare parts, training, and support to sustain operations and efficiently use information sources to focus their resources on threats."[1] The history of recent wars supports this conclusion.

Lebanon

A comparison of the inventories of Israel and Syria in 1982 suggests a fairly equal balance between them, with Israel maintaining only a slight edge. True, in helicopters the Israelis outnumbered the Syrians (187 to 150), but in tanks the Syrians had the advantage (3,990 to 3,140), and in combat planes they were about equal. (See appendix 2.) The relative age of Israeli and Syrian equipment was not too different either. On average the Israeli planes and helicopters were 13.3 and 14.6 years old respectively, in contrast to the approximately 15-year vintage of Syrian aircraft. Tanks differed by only about three years. (See table 9, p. 28.) How then to explain the outcome of the war and why the continuing operational disparity between Syrian and Israeli forces?

As described above, the majority assessment has been that it was not hardware but the Israeli use of well-executed battle management operations, effective tactics, and well-trained personnel able to improvise in the heat of battle that was responsible for their success.

Another view, however, cites the Israeli logistical system as deserving credit for the war's outcome – a factor rarely mentioned in evaluations of Israel's performance.[2] It holds that Israeli defense planners had learned from their experience in 1973, when only six divisions could be fielded and supplied for about 14 days. By 1982, they had effected a remarkable improvement in their capabilities and were organized not only to do battle but to supply an army of at least 11 divisions fighting at full strength for 28 days on three separate fronts.[3] But although logistical planning was critical, so too was its implementation. One commentator believes the performance of the Israeli engineers, whose mission it was to prevent the mountainous Lebanese terrain from hindering the advance and supply of the Israel Defense Forces (IDF), was particularly praiseworthy. He observes that

> In many ways the combat engineers were the unsung heroes of the war. Their actions in spanning rivers and rebuilding destroyed culvert bridges on narrow serpentine roads made it possible, in many instances, for the Israeli forces to continue to advance. Their cutting of flanking roads often contributed greatly to tactical victory and, at the same time, greatly reduced IDF casualties.[4]

To other analysts, however, the Lebanon war offers a classic example of inadequate preparation and training determining battle outcomes. In their opinion, the Israelis benefited as much from the omissions of the Syrians, as from their own martial skills. It was apparent, for instance, that the Syrians had not learned to refrain from turning on their radars until under direct attack and were unaware enemy aircraft could use them to home in on their antiaircraft emplacements.[5] They apparently left radars in operation unnecessarily, before and during the conflict, making it easier for the Israelis to identify and locate them. In addition, the Syrians did not take advantage of the mobility of the SA-6 missile launchers, leaving them vulnerable to attack by keeping them in place for long periods of time. These and a variety of other tactical errors are cited as largely responsible for their defeat.[6]

A year and a half later, the Syrian forces had done little to change this generally negative assessment. Western intelligence analysts asserted that Syrian troops were still far from an effective force. They were unable to use the new weapons delivered by the Soviet Union effectively and, perhaps even more important, to maintain them properly.[7] According to these estimates, the new arms supplied by the Soviets had not been assimilated into the Syrian military establishment and training courses had had little effect. Moreover, the logistics requirements of new equipment often had proven beyond the Syrian capabilities. For example, the delivery of large numbers of rocket launchers to Syria generated a demand for more trucks and drivers to transport the ammunition—not a major problem in Western armies, but in Syria trucks and drivers are commodities in short supply. In this situation, the lack of relatively basic support items had negative consequences for Syria's military readiness.[8]

According to many observers then, the Syrians seem generally unable to carry out modern infantry tactics, performing poorly in the field. Although capable of defense, the Syrian offensive capabilities have been minimal. As one Israeli officer said, "They are very good when they are dug in and have the clearly defined task of holding their ground. But they are much, much less effective when they have to climb out of their positions and maneuver under fire in the open field."[9] And another analyst concluded, "As for the success of the Soviet aid effort, the main problem is the human element . . . [in] the Syrian-Israeli balance. This will take three to five years at a minimum. . . . "[10] On both sides, then, human capabilities rather than technologies are credited with dictating victory.

İran-Iraq

The Iran-Iraq war provides another illustration of how human factors have affected the fortunes of recent wars. The Iranian air force once supported a vast array of U.S. aircraft. Since the revolution, however, its inventory of aircraft has been decimated, mainly because of lack of spare parts, a dearth of expert maintenance personnel, and attrition during its war with Iraq. One graphic description of the March 1985 battle for the Hawizah marshes observes that the Iranians were entirely without air support during this offensive.[11] In 1984 reportedly only 35–40 of Iran's combat aircraft were functioning. Other breakdowns suggest that of the 90 F-4s the Iranians once operated, fewer than 25 were serviceable and fewer than 30 F-5s were believed to be in flying condition.[12] Of the original 77 F-14s, only five were then thought to be operational, and they were not permitted to participate in direct air combat because of inadequately trained pilots. (Attrition by 1985 had undoubtedly reduced those numbers further.) Large numbers of helicopters also remained in storage due to serviceability problems.[13] Moreover, whatever level of operability had been attained is attributed to ground crews from other Third World countries, which have improved Iran's maintenance performance considerably since early 1983.

The situation is not easily remedied. Should the Iranian military decide to purchase Soviet or European aircraft, the aircraft will be of little utility until enough pilots and technicians have been trained. In sum, the human factor has determined the performance of Iran's air force, not the sophistication of its inventory. The same can be said for its ground forces, which have relied less on weapons and more on the fanatic devotion of its soldiers for assaults on the Iraqis.

In contrast, Iraq in 1984 was estimated to have more

than 500 combat aircraft in its inventory. But, according to MILAVNEWS of August 1983, despite its numerical superiority and the continuing deliveries of French and Soviet aircraft, Iraq has been incapable of using its aerial supremacy to good effect because of lack of an air-integrated battle plan as well as inadequate maintenance capabilities.

On the ground, Iraq's numerical advantage in armor also has proved of little use. After successfully sending its troops into Iran on September 2, 1980 and meeting with only small impromptu resistance groups, the Iraqi military temporized, digging in instead of advancing and taking advantage of the element of surprise and the disarray of the enemy. By spring 1981, the Iranians were sufficiently well organized to build defenses and, by September 1981, to launch an offensive that turned the tide of the war. In the spring of 1982, Iran regained its lost territory and by the following summer had carried the war to Iraq itself. Iraq's army, insufficiently trained and untried in the tactics of war and relying upon its numerical superiority in weapons as well as dissension within Iran to counterbalance these deficiencies, was unable to defeat the poorly equipped but fervently motivated Iranians.

The result has been a stalemated ground war with high attrition, which, at the level it is being fought, can continue indefinitely, barring financial exhaustion or domestic upheaval in one of the belligerents. Thus far comparative strength and technological advantage have had little influence on its progress. If anything, Iran, with its deteriorating force structure and continuing supply and logistics problems, has been surprisingly resilient. Some U.S. analysts believe, perhaps cynically, this is due, at least in part, to the continued presence of U.S.-trained technical personnel, such as the *Homofars*, in the Iranian armed forces.[14] Others attribute the Iranian performance in part to U.S.-trained military officers. One report, for example, maintains that the remnants of the regular military originally trained in U.S. facilities have been helping to coordinate battle plans.[15]

But whether U.S. training is partially responsible or not, clearly another human factor – morale and religious fervor – has contributed much to Iran's war effort. Unlike Iraq, Iran

has been able to draw upon an apparently inexhaustible supply of manpower. Even civilian casualties are absorbed as a
sacrifice to the Islamic revolution. In late 1984 there were
reports of some growing internal dissatisfaction, but by
spring 1986 they were not significant enough to bring Iran
to the negotiating table.

Ethiopia-Somalia

The relationship between technology and the human factor
has not been very different in another, less affluent region
of the world, the Horn of Africa. Despite the large deliveries
of matériel to Ethiopia, the Soviets found the Ethiopians
incapable of stemming the Somali invasion of the Ogaden.
The Ethiopians were so involved in their own internal problems and unfamiliar with Soviet technology that there was
little hope of victory without Soviet and Cuban intervention.
During the crucial battle for the city of Harar in January-
February 1978, Ethiopian troops were joined by 10–12 thousand Cubans led by a Soviet general, who had previously
headed the Soviet military mission to Somalia. A well-executed counteroffensive, based on the Soviet strategy of
outflanking the Somalis, finally halted the Somali advance.[16]

For Somalia, the situation in February 1977 was not
dissimilar to Iraq's in 1980. The Soviet-supplied Somali inventory in all categories of weapon systems outnumbered
Ethiopia's two or three to one. (See appendix 2.) In addition,
the Ethiopian regime was preoccupied with the Eritrean
revolt and with solidifying its domestic position after the
1974 coup that had deposed Emperor Haile Selasse. To the
Somalis, the time for battle must have seemed very auspi-
cious. Although many factors are said to have contributed
to the Somali defeat – Soviet and Cuban participation, the
U.S. refusal to aid Somalia, Somalia's lack of financial resources to buy arms elsewhere, the huge Soviet supply effort
on behalf of the Ethiopians – there still is a general consensus
among military observers that strategy and tactics, not numbers, won the day.[17]

In addition, the poor operational, maintenance, and logistics capabilities of Somalia turned what might have been temporary military reverses into total defeat. With Soviet military assistance to Somalia cut off, spares, maintenance, and servicing became a major problem. Inadequate logistical support for artillery and armored units impaired the Somalis' efforts to seize Harar and Diredawa and denied air support to Somali ground troops. Apparently the rudimentary Somali logistical system was simply incapable of supporting a conventional attack.[18] In the battle for Harar, for example, the supply and communications lines, based on the northern Somali city of Hargeisa, were hundreds of miles away and clearly overstretched, so that the regular Somali forces and the Western Somali Liberation Front guerrillas who were fighting with them were easily cut off from resupply by the Ethiopians.[19] And this was the norm rather than the exception. In addition to lack of air support, the Somalis were forced to abandon hundreds of tanks because of breakdowns and lack of spares or fuel. By February 1978, one year after they had initiated the war, the Somali air force had virtually ceased to operate, some of its aircraft having been shot down, but others having been grounded for lack of maintenance.[20] Thus, on the Somali as well as the Ethiopian side, the human factor had important consequences for both the course of battle and its outcome.

Central America

The United States has been faced with similar problems in El Salvador. Since 1979, in spite of U.S. military and economic assistance, infusions of matériel, intensive U.S. training, and a three or four to one manpower advantage, El Salvador's army has been unable to defeat the insurgents, the Farabundo Marti National Liberation Front, who are now active in 9 of the country's 14 provinces and have enlarged areas they contest or control.[21] And they have grown in number, from several hundred in the early 1970s to approximately 10 thousand in 1984.[22]

Several reasons for El Salvador's poor military performance have been offered by various observers, all of them
citing human rather than technological deficiencies. A U.S.
Senate report found that many of the Salvadorans being
trained had "trouble reading maps, were barely educated, and
were not aggressive enough."[23] In the army, logistics were
reputedly so snarled that troop morale was sagging from lack
of simple items such as ponchos and boots, and some troops
were defecting, seeking refuge in nearby villages while on
maneuvers.[24] According to military observers, the army's
tactics were deficient as well. They complained that too often
the Salvadorans reacted instead of taking the war to the insurgents, although reports in 1984 indicated that the army's
new quick reaction units may have become more active and
effective.[25]

The Salvadoran air force has not been exempt from these
problems. From published reports it is not clear whether El
Salvador has been losing more aircraft and helicopters to
enemy fire than to inexperienced pilots and ill-maintained
equipment.

Furthermore, according to some observers, the Salvadoran government's policy has been inconsistent, hampering
rather than assisting the war effort. In their view, government services, as well as external assistance programs, have
not been coordinated with a national military strategy. As
one Latin American specialist maintains, for these programs
to be effective in an insurgency "it requires an infrastructure,
communications links, secure areas, and a sympathetic population in the areas of conflict."[26] On the other hand, the Sandi-
nista-supported insurgents operating in El Salvador have
been given better performance marks, not because of their
weapons, but because they were "politically committed fighters who have organized public support and waged a war based
on genuine grievances."[27]

The charge of human failings has been leveled at the
Contra insurgents as well as the Salvadoran government. In
1986 one report claimed the "main Nicaraguan rebel force is
in its worst military condition since its formation in 1982."[28]

Although part of the problem was attributed to lack of appropriate weapons, the major failure was low morale and lack of direction. Officials say the Contras need a "thorough retraining in how to wage a guerrilla war and new tactics, including a political program that the rebels understand and can explain to the Nicaraguans." Even with such help, U.S. officials estimate it might take two more years for the rebels to become a real fighting force.[29]

In Central America, as in the Middle East and Africa, human rather than technological factors ultimately have had a decisive impact on the progress of war, as they undoubtedly will on its outcome.

Afghanistan

The Afghanistan war perhaps best illustrates the importance of training and morale in determining the choice of weapon transfers as well as the character and progress of the war.

After the coup against the Daoud government by pro-Soviet groups in April of 1978, major opposition to the new regime of Noor Mohammad Taraki began in October. In 1979 the Soviets began sending major weapons into the country, specifically helicopter gunships (Mi-24s) and armored cars, personnel carriers, BMPs (amphibious combat vehicles that can be dropped by parachute), BTR-152s (old armored personnel carriers), and some artillery and antiaircraft guns.[30]

But the Afghan military was a declining, demoralized force. Desertions, large scale surrenders to guerrillas, and serious shortages of replacements for weapons and of spare parts has reduced the Afghan government force to perhaps a quarter of its former effectiveness. Since 1980, desertions and casualties have reportedly reduced the Afghan army to 40 thousand men, less than half of its preinvasion strength of 100 thousand in 1977 and 1978.[31] As a result, much of the equipment the rebels have acquired has come from defeated or defecting government soldiers. Attrition due to mounting battle losses and desertions have been compounded by poor maintenance practices within the army.[32]

The Soviets, worried about Afghan troop loyalty and disheartened by their military performance, have disarmed many of them. At the beginning of the war, some government troops were so inexperienced that even the standard Communist issue, the AK-47 Kalashnikov rifle was giving them (and the rebels who captured some) jamming difficulties. According to one report, this was due to inadequate training and haphazard maintenance.[33] As one commentator observed at that time, "The army's contribution to the Soviet pacification effort well may be limited to providing guides."[34]

Since 1981, the Soviets have transferred relatively large amounts of equipment to Afghanistan for their own use, while keeping tight control over the Afghan army's inventory. After several years of experience, some of the early operational difficulties may have been eliminated, but morale problems have continued to plague the Afghan military. According to one 1984 account, because of the unreliability of Afghan troops "conscripts now have to wait up to six months before they are trusted with a gun," and the Soviets have gone so far as to remove the DShK 12.7-mm machine guns mounted on the Afghan army's T-55s to keep them from falling into rebel hands.[35]

The Soviets have made a particularly great effort to win over the Afghan air force. Conditions within the air force were not very different from those in the army during the early years of the war. As the situation continued to deteriorate, the Soviets were forced to play a larger role, often flying the MiG-21s and Mi-24s in the Afghan inventory.[36] Given the cost of the aircraft and their increasing role in the war against the rebels, the Soviets decided on an intensive training program to create a loyal cadre of pilots, one that would be capable of efficient operation and would not desert with their planes. About 7,000 Afghan officers and men are said to have received extensive political training.[37] Whether or not these men have been used in combat situations, and if so, whether their performance has improved, is unknown.[38] But the Soviet response is indicative of the importance they attach to the human factor in war.

Opposing the Afghan government and the Soviets are the Afghan rebels, who are even less tutored than the government soldiers in either the sophisticated arts of war or modern technologies. As a quarrelsome and warring lot, however, they are accustomed to mountain fighting and to the World War I vintage English Enfield rifles that they have been using for hunting game and each other for generations. Until recently, the Enfield was the rebel's weapon of choice because of its familiarity, minimal maintenance requirements, and its long barrel, which made it more accurate than the AK-47. Furthermore, spare parts and ammunition were readily available from the cottage industries in the North West Frontier area where the rifles are fabricated.[39] Even before the infusion of newer equipment from abroad and from local Soviet-supplied stores, these simple weapons had done a creditable job of tying down the Soviets and demoralizing government troops.

Since the Soviet invasion of Afghanistan, the CIA has overseen the transfer of military equipment to the Afghan guerrillas. Supplies have consisted of relatively simple, light, portable Soviet-made equipment (or replicas) such as rocket-propelled antitank grenades (RPG), mortars, the Kalashnikov AK-47 rifles, mines, grenade launchers, and machine guns — items untraceable to their real suppliers and supportable from stolen stores. Former Senator Birch Bayh, explaining U.S. policy in 1981, stated, "The objective was to strike a balance. On the one hand we wanted the Soviets to pay a significant price. On the other hand we didn't want to raise the conflict to the level of conventional warfare . . . or provide so much assistance that the Soviets would pour more troops in."[40]

But even at this level of transfer, extensive training was necessary, and training facilities in Pakistan were established to teach the rebels how to operate and maintain equipment as well as the basics of tactics, command structure, and the need for discipline.[41] As late as November 1982, almost two years after the weapons began arriving, the locally produced Enfield rifle reportedly remained the standard firearm of the

Afghan rebel.[42] By early 1984, however, one observer noted that "their personal weapon is the ubiquitous Kalashnikov AK-47 assault rifle, although there are many old Lee-Enfield .303s still in use."[43]

As the war has progressed, various attempts to introduce more complex weapons quickly have been unsuccessful. Each new system has required time and training before it has been absorbed by the rebel units. When the SA-7 Grail infrared guided surface-to-air missiles first arrived, probably in late 1981, they were ineffective because the mujaheddin were unable to install or use them correctly. The same proved true for the older ZU-23 air defense guns.[44] It was not until mid-1984 that there was some evidence they were being used effectively. By then, according to one source, the Soviets were suffering extensive helicopter and MiG losses and had been forced "to switch to high altitude bombing in Afghanistan as a response to the rebels' Soviet-made missiles and anti-aircraft guns."[45] Thus, time, experience, and training in the tactics, operations, and maintenance of newer weapons have been necessary before they could be efficiently absorbed and effectively utilized.

If there is a lesson to be learned about military assistance from this kind of insurgency, it is the importance of matching technologies and training to the skill level of the combatant. For the Afghan insurgents, technological simplicity has been the hallmark of success. The best form of military aid has been the kind of equipment they know and can support from their own or enemy stores.[46] Even though the systems obtained by the rebels are older and, by Western criteria, relatively unsophisticated, the rebels have been doing well on the battlefield. As early as 1983 the Pentagon concluded that the Soviet Union could not win its battle against the insurgents despite the increase in Soviet force levels. "Moscow is unable to control the Afghan countryside or to install a regime whose influence extends more than a few miles from major population centers."[47] And Secretary of Defense Caspar Weinberger observed, "There's more of Afghanistan that is under the control of the freedom fighters now than when the Soviets started."[48] The poor morale of the Afghan government soldiers and Soviet troops and the high motivation of the rebels, combined with their hit-and-run tactics, have been cited as the major reasons for the latter's relative success – not the technological sophistication of their arms.[49]

Morocco

The Moroccan experience provides a different lesson. It demonstrates how a government faced with an insurgency and fighting with demoralized troops and inadequate resources can, with tactical ingenuity, turn the tide of war. In early 1977, Morocco regarded certain technologies as vital to its war effort against the Polisario guerrillas in the Western Sahara. At issue were Cobra helicopter gunships and OV-10 reconnaissance planes, as well as a network of sensors (code named Westwind) that the Carter administration refused to sell for almost three years before finally relenting in October 1979.[50] (The latter two systems had been successfully employed in Vietnam.)

As it turned out, it was not just the new technologies but the resourceful defensive tactics and strategy that were initiated that changed the course of the war. Faced with a mobile, well-armed enemy, the Moroccans realized they could not, without great cost, hold the whole of the vast, almost empty Western Sahara even if the Great Powers were to be more forthcoming with arms. By constructing a 1,550-mile sand and stone wall, the Moroccan army was able to protect the "useful triangle" of the northern Sahara, which contains the major population centers and valuable phosphate deposits, leaving the rest of the barren desert (about the size of Colorado) and a long logistical support line to the guerrillas.

This 10-foot-high barrier wall has moved slowly south from Morocco's border with Algeria in the northeast and then west along the Mauritanian frontier to the Atlantic since its construction began in late 1980. It rises behind a ditch of the same depth. Barbed wire or electrified fencing stretch along the top, which is heavily fortified with strong points and electronic detection sensors. The strong points, spaced at about two-mile intervals, provide overlapping crossfire to intercept any Polisario guerrillas who manage to reach the wall. In 1984, the Polisario claimed control of two-thirds of the Western Sahara. By fall 1985, with the completion of the last segment of the wall, Western specialists estimated that the guerrillas held less than one-third.[51]

In the view of some military experts, because of Morocco's change in tactics and strategy the war is virtually over.[52] Rapid hit-and-run guerrilla strikes are no longer possible, and the Polisario's armored columns, stretched thin across the Western Sahara from their sanctuaries in Algeria and Mauritania, are easy prey to Moroccan attack helicopters. As of early 1986, the last major battle had occurred in October 1984.

The construction of the wall was accompanied by an aggressive political campaign on the part of King Hassan designed to isolate the guerrillas. The Libyan-Moroccan union agreement, for example, signed August 1984, deprived the Polisario of an important source of arms.[53] Since then Libya has ceased arms shipments to the guerrillas. Time is believed to be on the side of King Hassan. The vast empty desert spaces have little value, and when the Polisario and their backers tire, as some believe they will, the rest of the Western Sahara will fall to Morocco.[54] After years of conflict, however, the situation is still far from stable. The costs of the war have wreaked havoc with the Moroccan economy, and the government must now deal with increasing domestic unrest.

Vietnam-PRC

What little is known about the Vietnam-PRC war suggests its outcome, too, was decided less by the weapons employed than by "softer" factors. As we have seen in chapter 4, it was probably the Chinese, more than the Vietnamese, who were "taught a lesson" from the confrontation. Apparently the Vietnamese simply allowed the Chinese to lurch forward slowly with large numbers of antiquated weapons and untried troops and then to withdraw when they could no longer be

supported logistically.[55] For the Chinese, the experience highlighted their limitations in a variety of areas—command,
control, communications and intelligence (C³I); tactics; and
trained manpower. But according to some U.S. observers, the
war demonstrated most sharply the PRC's inability to provide adequate support for operations in a distant theater.[56]

A combination of too few trucks and an inadequate road
system in southern China created a transportation bottleneck
so intractable that at various times the PLA ran short of
ammunition, fuel, and rations. In time-honored fashion, the
PLA was forced to use human porters to deliver supplies up
to the PRC-Vietnam border. Furthermore, the PLA medical
system proved inadequate to the task and was unable to
evacuate rapidly or treat the high numbers of wounded. As
one analyst observed, "logistics was an area in which the
Chinese learned some very important lessons the hard way."[57]

As a consequence of the war, some modernization attempts are under way in both countries.[58] But for the PRC,
despite severe economic constraints, improving military readiness has become a matter of some urgency. In response to
this need, China has been attempting to rationalize its military, and there have been reports that military commanders
and political leaders are now debating how to update China's
military tactics. In addition, the Chinese are shopping for
new technologies and training services. Persistent rumors
suggest that Israeli technicians are currently in China in
various training and advisory capacities—about 200 are reported to be helping the Chinese upgrade their Soviet arms
with other Western technologies.[59]

But U.S. officials are not optimistic about China's ab-
sorptive capacity, particularly for modern technology. The
lack of trained personnel and skilled technicians is expected
to hinder severely the military's modernization efforts. As
on military specialist commented, "In a country where
a quarter of the population can't read, and where educational standards for the rest are low, I find it hard to imagine
the PLA operating modern weapons, even if they are home

made."[60] Others concur with this assessment. One Pentagon estimate concluded that because China's common soldier is still technologically unsophisticated, not only would the PLA have difficulty integrating more advanced U.S. systems into its force structure, but even less sophisticated equipment would rapidly deteriorate if proper maintenance were not adequately understood and performed.[61] Just as human skills decided the operations and outcome of the 1979 border war, so too are they deciding the pace and extent of China's military modernization.

The Falklands

Had arms transfer restrictions not been imposed, the Falklands war might have been an exception to the general human factor rule. But because of the embargo, Argentina lacked, and was unable to acquire, important technologies necessary to fight the war. Although Argentina's imported aircraft — the French-built Mirages, Israeli Neshers (Daggers), and U.S. A-4 Skyhawks that made up the bulk of its striking force — were good aircraft flown by competent crews, they lacked drop tanks and air-to-air refueling equipment to extend their range, without which Argentine pilots were able to do little more than one low-level attack before returning to base. Assessments of the Falklands war concur that this lack of air-refueling devices as well as the dearth of other items such as antisubmarine warfare systems, all-weather fighting capabilities, airborne reconnaissance and early warning facilities, and secure communications were all-important factors contributing to Argentina's defeat.[62] It is difficult to judge how the war might have ended had Argentina had access to more sophisticated aerospace technologies. Had that happened, it is possible that the ground war, in which the human factor heavily favored the British, might never have taken place.

As the war progressed, however, poor logistics, low morale, an absence of operational and tactical coordination, and inadequate training were as responsible for Argentina's defeat as high morale, disciplined soldiers, effective logistics, and integrated tactics were for the British victory.[63] Despite the enormous amount of attention given in the press to the balance of forces and the comparative capabilities of various weapon systems used in the war, men not matériel made the difference. Interservice rivalries prevented the three Argentine services from cooperating with each other in combat. Each in turn made serious errors of strategic judgment and operational performance. Even in the air, where well-trained and motivated Argentine pilots were involved, tactical miscalculations are thought to have contributed to Argentina's defeat. According to one British account, Argentina seemed incapable of organizing large raids on the British convoy, using its aircraft in small numbers that were never able to saturate British air defenses. In addition, the Argentine commanders decided to attack the heavily armed escorts to the British landing ships and not the unarmed landing ships themselves. "By wasting its strength against the covering naval units, the Argentine air force lost the chance to inflict decisive damage on the irreplaceable amphibious elements."[64]

On the ground the most important ingredient of Britain's victory was the vastly superior quality of its soldiers and their cohesion under fire. This was aided and abetted by Argentina's problem with logistics, that is, the difficulties the government had in supplying not only support equipment but also food to its troops in the Falklands. A report compiled by Major General Ernesto Crespo, chief of staff of the Argentine Air Force, concludes that "a lack of training in the Malvinas theatre" and "low combat morale" were largely responsible for the army's disastrous performance."[65] As one military analyst has written,

> In stark contrast to Argentina's poorly trained, wretchedly supplied, and indifferently led conscripts, British ground forces assigned to retake the Falklands consisted of superbly trained, long-service (three to 22 years) pro-

fessional troops. . . . The resulting contest on the ground was never in doubt.[66]

One cumulative lesson learned from these wars is that no amount of weaponry can substitute for motivated and well-trained manpower, and based on the evidence presented here, they are in generally short supply within Third World armies. This includes not only the men who operate the tanks, ships, and planes but those who service and maintain them — and the officers who manage, coordinate, and plan for war.

This discussion has not meant to suggest that weapons are unimportant to the conduct and outcome of Third World wars. Clearly, Iraq's superiority in the air and in armored vehicles has prevented its defeat, the helicopters and sensors shipped to Morocco have made a difference in the Western Sahara, and the war in Lebanon would have lasted longer, inflicting higher casualties on the Israelis had they not possessed modern command and control and surveillance systems. The point is that in recent wars it has not been weapons that have given the victor the edge.

New weapons that have promised enhanced capabilities often have burdened the Third World recipient with requirements for infrastructure and for maintenance, logistical, and operational skills that are rarely available. Often additions to inventory have called for changes in tactics and doctrine as well, changes requiring time, training, and foreign advisory assistance. Modern weapon transfers to LDC combatants have not, therefore, translated into short-term military power and have instead increased the combatants' dependency upon long-term training in operational and maintenance techniques and the donors that can supply them.[67] Judging from recent wars, if modern weapons are to be assimilated into LDC inventories, years rather than months of preparation will be necessary. One wonders, of course, whether styles of combat are not culturally determined — whether they are not as deeply ingrained in society as the language people speak and the kind of food they eat. If so, the process of acculturation to

Western weapons may take a very long time indeed and may never be completely successful.[68]

The Expense of Weapons and Wars

Financial Constraints on Combatants

A second major constraint on the war-fighting capabilities of LDCs, one often overlooked in the literature, is the expense of wars. Few countries can afford long wars – and even those fighting short wars require extensive resupply such as Syria after the Lebanon war. It is estimated, for example, that the Falklands were liberated at a cost to Britain of $1.2 billion, or about $665 thousand per Falkland resident.[69] And in Argentina, after the disastrous Falklands invasion that ended with more than $800 million lost just in military equipment, social unrest over the economic situation forced the new government to reduce its military procurements.[70] The three-week war between the PRC and Vietnam is said to have cost the PRC between $3.2 and $6.4 billion. The price of the Lebanon invasion for Israel was $1 billion in direct costs between June 1982 and the end of 1984, and this does not include the indirect costs of calling up reserves from the civilian economy.[71]

Estimates for long wars still under way are generally more difficult to obtain, and what is published is usually an aggregate figure or the average yearly outlay. There is, therefore, no way of knowing whether wars become more or less expensive to fight the longer they continue. As in the case of short wars, some long wars have been dearer than others. For example, in 1984 Morocco was reportedly spending between about $350 million and $550 million per year on the war over the Western Sahara, whereas in Afghanistan, the Soviets are said to be spending between $2–$5 billion per year on the insurgency.[72] In the Middle East, the Iran-Iraq war is thought to be costing Iran approximately $11 billion a year.[73] No estimates are available for Iraq although their need for outside financial support (discussed below) suggests a heavy burden.

In addition to the enormous expense of fighting and supplying a war, most LDCs are laboring under large foreign debts, which are exacerbated by the demands of armed conflict. It is interesting in this regard, and contrary to the expectations of the author, that foreign debt and war were not correlated for the combatants examined here. Clearly, as table 11 indicates, long wars have created a larger burden for governments than short wars, with the debt/gross national product (GNP) ratio rising more steeply for the latter than the former. Thus for countries fighting long wars the debt ratio rose 121 percent as opposed to 43 percent for short-war combatants. But LDCs fighting long wars did not necessarily owe more to foreign lenders than their more peaceful neighbors. In fact, they owed less. This finding holds for all the combatants. Note in table 11 that at the end of 1982 none of the belligerents have debt ratio's as high as Mauritania's, and only Nicaragua and Israel ranked second and eighth among the 10 largest debtor nations in the world per GNP. Honduras takes tenth place with all the rest falling below.[74] As a group, the percent increase of debt for combatants rose less sharply than that for noncombatants (+94 percent change as opposed to +173 percent change), and even the debt for states involved in long wars rose more slowly (+121 percent change) than the cumulative debt of the noncombatants.

But although war does not necessarily create large foreign debts, it exacerbates them, and war-associated military expenditures become more difficult to bear. The significance for the LDCs has been that few can afford to pay the costs of war and they are therefore increasingly dependent upon the largesse of others to finance them. For Third World states, as the price for fighting wars has climbed, conducting them without outside financial assistance has become difficult if not impossible.

Similarly, for donor states, the burden of supplying the military needs of friends and allies has become increasingly heavy. As table 12 indicates, many LDCs require subsidies

TABLE 11
Total Foreign Debt as Percent of GNP (U.S. $ millions)

Combatants	1972			1975			1982		
	Debt[1]	GNP[2]	%	Debt[3]	GNP[2]	%	Debt[4]	GNP[2]	%
Short Wars									
Argentina	2424.1	56158.0	4.32	1333.7	77010.0	1.73	15780.0	120344.0	13.11
PRC	na	172000.0E	na	1694.7	271000.0E[+]	0.63	6397.0E[**]	698000.0	0.92
Vietnam	95.8	1221.0E	7.85	1100.0[+++]	1281.0E[+]	85.87	978.0E[*]	8600.0[++]	11.37
Syria	161.8	3816.0	4.24	660.7	7020.0	9.41	2616.1	17583.0	14.88
Israel	3585.8	8398.0	42.70	6828.0	11855.0	57.60	14899.5	22917.0	65.02
% average			14.78			31.05			21.06
% change[5]			+110.08			−32.17			
				+42.49					

(continued)

Long Wars

Ethiopia	226.9	1742.0	13.03	381.3	2296.0	16.61	874.6	4635.0	18.87
Somalia	106.6	734.0	14.52	265.9	958.0	27.76	944.0	1985.0	47.56
Morocco	894.1	5071.0	17.63	1593.4	7767.0	20.51	9030.4	16906.0	53.42
Iran	225.6	25078.0E	0.90	4617.2	65205.0E	7.08	3433.0E*	84660.0E***	4.05
Iraq	406.6	4915.0E	8.27	596.0	14177.0E	4.20	4496.0E*	25177.0E	17.86
Afghanistan	679.2	1109.0	61.24	786.6	1766.0	44.54	277.0E*	2400.0E***	11.54
Nicaragua	218.1	1161.0	18.79	600.0	1786.0	33.59	2810.0	2515.0	111.73
El Salvador	109.3	1578.0	6.93	204.9	2329.0	8.80	801.3	3496.0	22.92
Honduras	119.3	902.0	13.23	272.7	1164.0	23.43	1384.8	2587.0	53.53
% average			17.17			20.72			37.94
% change[5]		+20.68			+120.97			+83.11	

Total Combatants

% average	16.43	24.41	31.91
% change[5]	+48.57	+94.22	+30.73

93

TABLE 11
(Continued)

Combatants	1972			1975			1982		
	Debt[1]	GNP[2]	%	Debt[3]	GNP[2]	%	Debt[4]	GNP[2]	%
Noncombatants[6]									
Mauritania	35.4	288.0	12.29	188.1	361.0	52.11	1000.7	747.0	133.96
(Nicaragua)									(111.73)
Togo	45.9	349.0	13.15	119.8	493.0	34.30	819.0	918.0	89.22
Zaire	576.6	2623.0	21.98	1718.4	3460.0	49.66	4118.4	5395.0	76.33
Congo	156.6	507.0	30.89	373.9	786.0	47.57	1369.9	1970.0	69.54
Panama	284.5	1249.0	22.78	770.7	1747.0	44.12	2820.4	4035.0	69.90
Guinea	489.5	627.0	78.07	761.8	882.0	86.37	1229.9	1685.0	72.99
(Israel)									(65.02)
S. Yemen	49.0	873.0	5.61	98.9	1443.0	6.85	760.5	3636.0	20.92
Jamaica	147.8	1726.0	8.56	688.3	2134.0	32.25	1511.1	2951.0	51.21
Liberia	155.5	397.0	39.17	175.7	481.0	36.53	641.2	976.0	65.70
Egypt	1580.8	6478.0	24.40	3639.7	9263.0	39.29	14935.2	29375.0	50.84
% average			25.69			42.91			70.06
% change[5]			+67.03			+63.27			
					+172.71				

1. *World Debt Tables*, International Bank for Reconstruction and Development (IBRD), 1974–1975.

2. ACDA, *World Military Expenditures and Arms Transfers*, 1972–1982.

3. IBRD, *World Debt Tables*, 1976–1977.

4. IBRD, *World Debt Tables*, 1983–1984.

5. Taking 1972 as the base year from which the percent changes are calculated.

6. The noncombatant countries chosen are those with the highest Debt/GNP ratio for 1979 as listed in the George T. Kurian, *New Book of World Rankings* (New York: Facts on File, 1984).

⁺Estimate for 1978, ACDA, *WMEAT*, 1972–1982.

⁺⁺Ruth Leger Sivard, *World Military and Social Expenditures: An Annual Report on World Priorities* (Washington, D.C.: World Priorities, 1983).

⁺⁺⁺1978 Figure

*OECD Estimate 1983.

**IMF Estimate 1983.

***1981 Estimate, IISS, *Military Balance*, 1984–5.

E Estimate

TABLE 12
Grant/Discount on Military Assistance Deliveries
A Comparison of Supply Patterns, 1954–1982/83 ($ millions)

	Total $ Value	% USSR Grant/ Discount	% Other Communist Grant/ Discount	% U.S. Grant/ Discount	% Other Western Grant/ Discount	% U.S. Grant/ Discount U.S. Program[a]	% USSR Grant/ Discount USSR Program[a]	% Total Grant/ Discount of Total $ Value
Argentina	3,009.3	0.0	0.0	3.8	0.0	34.1	0.0	3.8
El Salvador	141.3	0.0	0.0	49.8	0.0	75.9	0.0	49.8
Honduras	96.3	0.0	0.0	22.1	negl.	57.6	0.0	22.1
Nicaragua	255.7	50.6	9.2	9.4	1.2	71.8	131.8[b]	70.4
Morocco	2,906.8	0.5	0.03	4.4	6.4	18.9	29.9	11.3
Ethiopia	3,278.5	60.3	1.1	8.3	2.3	84.0	76.3	72.0
Somalia	1,171.3	10.0	0.4	2.6	54.9	49.5	29.1	68.0
Afghanistan	1,370.0	48.7	0.0	0.4	negl.	90.3	48.9	51.0
Israel	13,436.5	0.0	0.0	53.3	0.3	57.6	0.0	53.6
Syria	15,295.0	2.8	negl.	0.0	8.0[c]	0.0	3.3	10.8
Iraq	20,666.1	2.9	negl.	0.0	0.1	0.0	5.4	8.4
Iran	19,436.8	0.0	0.0	5.5	0.6	8.3	0.0	6.1
Vietnam	24,236.3	25.4	7.0	66.7	0.02	100.0	97.6	99.1
PRC	3,320.7	0.0	0.0	0.0	0.0	0.0	0.0	0.0

Source: DSAA, *Fiscal Yearbook, 1982; The Military Balance,* various years (London: IISS); U.S. government sources.

a. This represents the proportion of grant/discount to total U.S. or USSR military aid to the recipient: ($ Value of Grant/ Discount)/($ Value of U.S. (USSR) Military Aid to the Recipient).

b. The Soviet Union paid for transfers from other Communist countries.

c. Libya, Saudi Arabia, Algeria.

for more than 50 percent of their military purchases. The amount varies from 99.1 percent for Vietnam, to as little as 3.8 percent for Argentina – but for half of our sample of countries the ratio of financial concessions to aid is 50 percent or more.

Vietnam-PRC.   For example, Vietnam, a country that has been fighting wars since 1945 and that maintains an estimated 1 million troops (the world's fourth largest army after China, the Soviet Union, and the United States), has exhausted its economic resources and is now one of the poorest states in the world with a per capita income of $160. The Organization for Economic Cooperation and Development (OECD) estimates Vietnam's debt in 1983 as $978 million. Others have suggested the actual figure is much higher, but all agree that whatever the actual debt, it is so large that Vietnam cannot afford to pay the interest, much less the principal it owes.[75] Reportedly it has been necessary for the Soviet Union to pour $4–$5 million a day in economic and military aid into Vietnam to help keep it afloat.[76] Note that during the period 1954–1982/1983, 98 percent of the Soviet and 100 percent of the U.S. military assistance to Vietnam was subsidized. (See table 12.)

To repay its debts, Vietnam exports some food to the Soviet Union, and half a million Vietnamese laborers reportedly have gone to work in the USSR, East Germany, Czechoslovakia, and Bulgaria, where more than 60–75 percent of their pay is believed to be deducted to help reimburse Soviet aid.[77]

For the Soviets, Vietnam's increasing economic needs have become burdensome. The slowdown in the Soviet economy and their other costly involvements in Afghanistan, Poland, and Cuba meant cutbacks in their economic aid to Vietnam beginning early in 1980. As a result, economic issues have caused great friction in the Soviet-Vietnamese relationship, and there has been rising anti-Soviet feeling in Vietnam. The Vietnamese went so far as to declare at their Party Congress held in March 1982 that Vietnam should "endeavour to establish relations . . . with countries outside the socialist community."[78] But for the Vietnamese the prospect of defending themselves against their Chinese neighbor, without significant military and economic support from the Soviet Union, must be discouraging indeed. It may not be a coincidence that at the initiative of Vietnam in 1982, a cautious, if short-lived, Chinese-Vietnamese rapprochement began. But in early 1986, Vietnam was still as dependent as ever on Soviet economic aid.

In China, straitened financial circumstances have resulted in an antiquated inventory for the world's largest armed forces, with military doctrine that dates back to the 1950s. It has been said that PLA is "worse off today than it was in the 1950s."[79] Some observers are convinced that there is "no reason to believe that the PRC can project conventional military power any farther beyond its borders today than it could in 1950."[80] Reliable statistics on the state of the Chinese economy are not publicly available, but if the condition of its military and the indeterminate outcome of its invasion of Vietnam in 1979 are indicators, economic constraints have had a serious effect upon China's war-fighting capabilities. Modernization will require a large financial investment and dependence upon foreign suppliers for modern military technology.

El Salvador and Nicaragua.   In 1982, El Salvador's foreign debt widened to $800 million according to the International Bank for Reconstruction and Development (IBRD), or to $1.3 billion according to its Central Reserve Bank president.[81] U.S. aid reportedly accounts for nearly one-third of El Salvador's GNP – a GNP that has declined 25 percent in real terms since 1979. By the end of 1983, its foreign debt was reported equal to one-half its GNP.[82] Although the total dollar value of El Salvador's military procurement between 1954 and 1982 was not large ($141 million), 76 percent of its assistance from the United States has had to be subsidized, and the proportion is likely to increase in the future.

Nicaragua's economic dependence is even greater. Unable to pay its rising oil debt to Venezuela and Mexico, Nicaragua has become increasingly reliant upon the Soviet Union for petroleum imports as well as arms and economic assistance. Western diplomats estimate that Soviet economic aid reached $150 million in 1984, at least a 25 percent increase over 1983. Part of the aid package was oil. The Soviet Union probably provides about one-fourth of Nicaragua's oil, in addition to large amounts of wheat and almost all of its military equipment (although some of the latter arrives via third countries, such as Cuba and Libya.)[83] As table 12 indicates, more than 50 percent of Nicaragua's arms deliveries have been subsidized by the USSR.

Syria-Israel. For the non-oil rich combatants in the Middle East the picture is equally bleak. Syria, for example, to sustain its military posture in Lebanon has been dependent upon significant amounts of Arab economic aid. Under the Baghdad agreement of 1978, Arab nations agreed to give Syria $1.8 billion per year as a frontline state. In 1980, Libya alone reportedly sent $1 billion directly to the Soviet Union to finance Syrian arms purchases, in addition to a $600 million direct subsidy to Syria.[84]

This generous assistance program, much of it grant-aid, probably accounts for Syria's relatively low GNP/debt ratio (15 percent) in table 11. After the Lebanon war, financial aid apparently also permitted Syria to purchase arms from the Soviet Union without the need for major loans, credits, discounts, or grants. Much of the $2.5 billion Soviet resupply effort after the conflict was financed by Saudi Arabia.[85]

But in spite of continuing Saudi support, Syria's economic situation worsened. In 1981 and 1982, total Arab aid dropped to between $1–1.2 billion per year, and by 1983 it had fallen below $1 billion.[86] The slack has apparently been taken up by Iran. Iran is now reportedly providing Syria with as much, and probably more, than the Saudis. Iranian aid (primarily oil subsidies) is estimated at $1 billion per year and Saudi Arabian donations at about $800 million. The grant-aid portion of the Iranian subsidy may be as high as $600 million annually. The Syrian contribution to this relationship of mutual convenience is Soviet arms given to Iran and the closing of Syria's pipeline to Iraqi oil (despite pleas to the contrary from other Arab states), depriving Iraq of the revenues from 1.2 million barrels of oil a day.[87]

To date, Syria has been completely dependent upon outside sources for financial assistance. But the size of its subsidies is apparently diminishing. By 1983, Syria reportedly could no longer afford to pay cash for all its military imports. Instead it paid 25 percent, taking long-term loans for the rest.[88] If its resources and those of its financial supporters continue to decline, the implications for Syria's military capabilities, already limited, are not promising, and its domestic stability may be even more disastrously affected.

Israel's economic condition is no less precarious and dependent. Israeli inflation has roller-coasted between approximately 500 percent and 1,000 percent between October 1982 and the end of 1984; in 1982 its foreign debt constituted 65 percent of its GNP.[89] From 1954–1982, Israel procured from abroad more than $13 billion worth of military equipment and training, of which about 54 percent represented concessional or grant-aid. The burden of assistance has rested primarily on the United States, Israel's principal supplier, which has provided grants-in-aid or discounts for 58 percent of its military assistance to Israel.

By 1984 the situation had become so desperate economically that the Israeli cabinet was forced to cut government expenditures by $600 million and reduce the defense budget by $169 million, the latter hitherto virtually sacrosanct.[90] The Israeli public's concern over the ailing economy and their reluctance to become further involved in Lebanon have considerably limited Israel's military options. To keep Israel actively engaged in the multinational pacification effort in Lebanon, the United States was forced to ease the pressure on Israel's economy by permitting much of the loan portion of $2.6 billion in military and economic aid to Israel to be converted to outright grants.[91] The problematic economic situation has continued, as has the need for increased U.S. aid.

On July 1, 1985, in part in response to U.S. prodding, Israel's government introduced a radical stabilization program designed to bring the inflation rate down to 20 percent or less a year.[92] How successful it will be over the long run is still being debated, but there is little question that in the immediate future financial constraints will affect the quantity if not the quality of Israeli procurements and its training capabilities.

Iraq-Iran. Even oil-rich states such as Iraq and Iran have had severe economic difficulties sustaining a long war. Recent assessments indicate that Iran has been spending 30 percent of its annual $36 billion budget on its war with Iraq, in part because of the West's embargo that compels Iran to pay up to three times the normal price for weapons imported through indirect sources.[93]

Despite reports about Iran's growing domestic military production capability for ammunition and some spares, Iran's constant need for resupply and its demand for more sophisticated items, combined with its apparent willingness to pay almost anything for them, have created an army of privateers who charge exorbitant prices. In one publicized case, six Americans accused of attempting to smuggle more than $75 million in advanced missiles and weapons to Iran apparently intended to charge 200–300 percent more than the missiles had cost them.[94] As oil revenues continue to fall and the oil glut grows larger, the cost of war is becoming a greater burden, and there are rumors that among the mullahs there is dissension over whether it is worth the price.[95]

For Iraq, the war has also had major economic consequences. The shutting down of Syria's pipeline to Iraqi oil, at Iran's request, left Iraq with only one outlet, the new Turkish pipeline. As a result, Iraqi oil exports were cut back sharply to one-fifth their prewar level, and oil revenues fell to less than one-third their prewar level.[96] Inflation, fueled by continued heavy spending for the war effort, rose to more than 40 percent, and a large foreign debt estimated at $4.5

billion, which requires servicing, has meant an austerity program that has cut development programs.[97] To compensate for oil revenue losses and bridge the financial gap, Iraq has increased its borrowing and turned to other Arab states for financial aid. By the end of 1982, Arab aid had reached $50 billion (including $30 billion from Saudi Arabia and $15 billion from Kuwait), approximately $20 billion of which went to pay for needed arms supplies.[98] By mid-1984, Iran claimed that Saudi Arabia's subsidies to Iraq had reached $1 billion per month.[99] Since 1983, the United States has also taken a number of steps to shore up the Iraqi economy. These include the provision of nearly $1 billion in commodity credits to facilitate Iraq's purchases of U.S. agricultural and other products and the decision of the Export-Import Bank to guarantee 85 percent of the $570 million required to construct a new pipeline to Aqaba.[100]

Ethiopia-Somalia.   In the Horn, Ethiopia and Somalia, often considered "basket cases" by the international financial community, are also heavily dependent upon outside sources of support for their military efforts. Sixty-eight percent of Somalia's arms-related purchases and 72 percent of Ethiopia's have been acquired via grant or concessional programs. In Ethiopia, the Soviet Union has borne 60 percent of the burden, and diversified Western countries primarily in the Arab world have subsidized 55 percent of Somalia's purchases.

Morocco.   Morocco's deteriorating economic situation has set exacting limits on what the government can and cannot afford to spend on arms. As early as 1976, one-third of Morocco's budget went for military expenditures, and by 1977 this had increased another 50 percent. Inflation then at 12.5 percent forced the king to cut food subsidies, which, in turn, precipitated strikes throughout the country.[101] By 1978, Morocco was dependent upon the Saudis for military funding. In 1981, although the war was going well, severe financial setbacks caused by its cost, staggering oil imports, a two-year drought that forced Morocco to increase its food imports by

76 percent, and a major balance of payments deficit aggravated by slumping prices in the world market for Morocco's principal export, phosphates, all necessitated an International Monetary Fund (IMF) standby credit of $988 million, reputed to be the second largest "rescue" in the Fund's history. Austerity conditions imposed by the IMF forced the government to raise basic food prices again and to continue its dependence upon foreign sources for military assistance.[102]

By 1982, Morocco's foreign debt was running about 53 percent of its GNP; France was forced to reschedule its former colony's $800 million debt to enable it to buy more arms, and a Saudi subsidy was underwriting 80 percent of Morocco's war effort.[103] The same year the Reagan administration allocated $30 million in military assistance and initiated a major development aid program, giving Morocco $200 million over five years—at least one-half of which went for repayment of debts.[104] Foreign borrowing took up the rest of the slack.

But despite these heroic measures, Morocco's economy continued to go from bad to worse. In 1983, Morocco's difficulties in repaying interest on its FMS debt led to warnings from the United States that all military and economic assistance might have to be stopped.[105] Today, few foreign banks will lend Morocco money, and falling oil revenues have led Saudi Arabia to reduce its subsidies substantially. Undoubtedly these economic woes had much to do with Morocco's union with Libya in August 1984. The union promised employment opportunities in Libya for Moroccan workers and foreign currency earnings, increased trade, and Libyan investments in Morocco's economy. But more important, it promised an end to Libya's arms transfers to the Polisario and the prospect of reducing Morocco's own military expenditures.

Financial Constraints on Insurgents

The same financial constraints and dependencies also characterize the war effort of insurgents. The Polisario are as dependent on outside financial support as is the Moroccan government. Both Algeria and Libya have been their main sources of aid. But in late 1982, Algeria, impatient with the financial and political cost of helping the guerrillas, began reducing its support and level of assistance. As a result, according to one assessment, Polisario victories declined after 1982, and offensives that were launched appear to have originated from Mauritania not Algeria. This assessment suggests that if the Polisario insurgents can no longer operate from their sanctuaries in Algeria, then they have only their bases in northern Mauritania as sanctuaries, and these are vulnerable to Moroccan air attack. Accordingly, in this view, the offensive capabilities of the Polisario have been considerably reduced.[106] More certain are the repercussions from Libya's defection from the Polisario cause, which not only has deprived the guerrillas of an important source of arms but of economic and political support as well.

Similar constraints face insurgents in other regions of the Third World. The PLO rearmament drive in 1978–1982 was subsidized by the Communist bloc, Libya, and some Arab states. But for the PLO, defeat in war was costly. Since 1982, its fortunes have declined in tandem with the dwindling economic and political support of its former donors. Of the former seven countries that pledged, in 1978, to contribute a total of $3 billion over 10 years to the PLO, some have reneged entirely and others partly. One report estimates that although the PLO's income from investments and contributions in 1985 totaled about $154 million, its expenses came to at least $310 million. Although still formally at war with Israel, the PLO would find launching another major rearmament effort is beyond the organization's economic and political capabilities without considerable outside assistance, which now is declining.[107]

In Afghanistan the rebels remain completely dependent upon outside sources to finance their activities, which reportedly cost $75 million annually in arms and aid.[108] The Afghan government claims that between 1981–1985 Saudi Arabia alone financed the transfer of over $400 million worth of equipment. But because of their reliance on outside sources for funds, the Afghan insurgents have not always been able to acquire the kinds of weapons they request, when they request them. As a result, they have frequently complained publicly about the pace and content of deliveries.

The Contras are equally reliant upon outside financing. But funding from their primary backer, the United States, has been inconstant, and at times they have had to contend with complete cutoffs. In 1984, the U.S. Congress ended military aid to the Contras, forcing them to rely on private donations until Congress granted them $27 million for non-lethal aid in 1985. Assistance from other sources has been equally unreliable, with countries such as Honduras suspending their aid in an effort to extract political concessions from the United States on other issues.[109] The result, according to the guerrilla leaders, has been a poorly equipped, demoralized insurgent movement.[110]

For all of the combatants in recent wars – the non-oil rich developing states, the insurgents, and the resource-rich LDCs – military capabilities have been constrained by economic factors. Given the price of sophisticated modern weapons, not to mention the expense of training men to use them, it is no coincidence that Third World states have relied heavily upon their ground forces to do battle, cautiously husbanding their more costly major naval vessels and aircraft. In all recent wars, LDC navies have been conspicuous by their modest operations or by their absence, and with the exception of Israel, Third World air forces have played a secondary role.[111] For the resource scarce LDCs, high attrition ground wars have proven expensive enough to maintain and resupply, and most have experienced great difficulty in doing so. The price has been dependence on others for the conduct of war.

A growing number of states seem to have drawn important lessons from the costly experience of combatants in recent wars and are beginning to change their buying habits. They are moving away from late-model weaponry, instead modernizing their existing inventory, or, when necessary, buying older upgraded items. To compensate for financial constraints as well as weaknesses in the human factor described above, less affluent countries are showing more interest in spending scarce resources on training, support services, and infrastructure, such as instruction in low-level maintenance, tactical training, and logistics; building up air, ground, and naval communications and a logistical infrastructure; accumulating war reserve supplies of consummables; improving C³I by investing in surveillance and reconnaissance training and hardware; increasing combat support capabilities through the purchase of transport aircraft, engineering equipment, tank transporters, and similar systems.[112] In response to the economic and human realities of war, more states are purchasing fewer items than those being phased out of inventory, in the hope that quality will compensate for quantity in deterring or fighting wars. Given the escalating costs of military technologies, this is probably a trend most LDCs will follow in the future.

The expense of war has had a crucial impact on its conduct and outcome. Like the human factor, it has helped determine the performance of the combatants in battle, their implements of war, and the degree to which they have been dependent upon outside powers for help. It is to the question of dependency that this paper now turns.

6

Dependency, Power, and Influence: The Role of Military Assistance

The previous chapters have examined patterns of superpower arms transfers and training to warring Third World states, the LDC trend toward increasing diversification of suppliers and indirect transfers, the role played by the combatants' indigenous defense industries, and the overall effectiveness of military assistance programs during recent wars. This chapter will attempt to evaluate the significance of these patterns for future relations between recipients and suppliers during combat.

The obvious increase in diversified procurement, the decline of monopolistic military assistance relationships, and the growing number of suppliers in the arms trade documented here and elsewhere have caused some observers to declare that superpower influence in the international system has been eroded. Fewer states, they argue, need to buy arms from the superpowers, thereby reducing the leverage of the latter and increasing the political and military independence of the former, especially during periods of regional conflict.

To all appearances, recent developments in the arms trade support this view. Economic factors have had and still are having the effect of fractionating the procurement practices of both combatant and noncombatant LDCs. Even in peacetime the rising expense of modern weapons designed and manufactured in the developed world is forcing poorer states to buy fewer, newer models. In both the United States and Soviet Union, each new generation of weapon is 3 to 10 times more expensive than that of its predecessor.[1] And this is true for items produced in other countries as well. Today one French Mirage 2000 sells for approximately $30 million, and even Israel's Lavi, a fighter currently in development, will have an estimated flyaway price of $22 million per copy.[2]

In response to this development, many LDCs are attempting to upgrade what is already in inventory or they are buying older equipment that has been modernized.[3] In turn, a large industry devoted to retrofitting and modernizing aging planes, missiles, and tanks has evolved to satisfy this demand. Facilities to upgrade both Western and Eastern systems have grown and expanded not only in the United States, but also in Israel and China. In recent years upgrading old Soviet equipment for countries that have broken relations with the USSR and are having difficulty maintaining their equipment has become a particularly big business, offering significant savings to LDC buyers. For example, U.S. companies are helping Egypt modernize its older Soviet technology. The Chinese are marketing a MiG with new avionics and some engine improvements for $10 million, in contrast to the nearest U.S. equivalent, which costs $13–$14 million. And the Israelis have retrofitted T-54 and T-55 Soviet tanks captured in battle with new cannons and laser range finders, which are available for $500 thousand compared to new German or U.S. battle tanks that sell for $2–$3 million.[4] Even Peru's Sukhoi (SU-22) fighters, purchased during the 1970s, have been retrofitted with U.S. electronic systems. The upgrade has proved so successful, an additional 16 aircraft of this type have been ordered.[5]

In addition, a rising number of states are now producing consumables to suit a wide variety of weapon systems – not just those in their own inventory. Converting production lines to manufacture different caliber small arms and artillery ammunition is not very difficult or expensive and can be accomplished within a few weeks. Therefore, as demand for consumables has risen in recent wars, so too have the facilities that produce them. North Korea, for instance, supplies Iran with ammunition compatible with the latter's U.S.-origin systems. And Bulgaria is reported to have provided NATO-standard ammunition to the Sandinistas in Central America.[6] Thus regardless of origin of design, Third World states now have many different sources available to turn to for improving their war-making.

Curiously, the arms trade is becoming more, rather than less, homogenized while it is growing increasingly fragmented, as more suppliers are able to provide compatible matériel across blocs. This is a growing trend – one that has developed from economic exigencies and one that will undoubtedly continue to be an important characteristic of the arms trade.

A careful analysis of the evidence from recent wars, however, suggests that diversity and homogenization have not necessarily changed the structure of the international arms transfer system. Despite these developments, the dependency of less industrialized states upon the superpowers appears to be increasing rather than decreasing. Although the procurement process is changing, these changes do not seem to have eroded superpower influence on, or preeminent position in, the arms trade. On the contrary, diversification of supply appears to enhance their influence, and, in some instances, even to be an outgrowth of it. A variety of constraints on recipients as well as other smaller suppliers has served to reduce the combatants' options and given the superpowers a good measure of control over the pattern of military assistance during combat.

Constraints on Recipients

The findings in previous chapters suggest that a variety of external and internal socioeconomic factors have been responsible for the combatants' limited access to military supplies during recent wars. First, the self-imposed resupply restraint of the superpowers has successfully capped the sophistication level of weapons available to combatants, by forcing many of them to resort to the covert gray market that traffics mainly in smaller, older military items. This equipment can sustain a ground war of attrition, but superpower control over the transfer of modern major systems has effectively circumscribed the antagonists' choice of matériel and ultimately, their offensive capabilities.

Second, even when more advanced systems have been made available, human factors have limited the war-fighting abilities of the recipients. As the Third World combatants have learned, high technology items are not easy to integrate into force structures nor are they simple to maintain in operational condition.[7] Most LDCs found that the transfer of advanced weapons not only reduced their war-fighting ability, but also increased their dependence on foreign suppliers for training, help in building infrastructure, and assistance in tactics, logistics, operations, management, and maintenance. In some instances, even the transfer of relatively simple military equipment required the logistical and support assistance of one of the superpowers.

Third, the indigenous production capacities of the combatants also proved inadequate to sustain their own war effort. Even Israel, with relatively advanced industrial skills, relied heavily on major foreign systems during the Lebanon war. Had the war continued at a high attrition rate longer than it did, Israel would also have had to turn to the United States for the resupply of many spare parts and munitions for those systems originating in U.S. industries.

Fourth, recent wars demonstrate the extent to which economics molds the capabilities of Third World countries, determining what and how much they can buy. Many donors may have arms to sell, but a combatant may not be able to pay for them, and small suppliers cannot afford to give generous credits or grants. Even major suppliers such as France are limited in the amount of economic assistance they can offer Third World buyers over the long term. Although some of the oil rich states are able to assist their friends and neighbors, they themselves are dependent upon one or the other of the superpowers for military equipment and support and are, therefore, susceptible to pressures from them to initiate or reduce arms supplies to LDC belligerents. Furthermore, as oil revenues have dwindled – in March 1986, oil prices fell below $12 a barrel – the amount of financial resources available to the Gulf states and Libya for disbursement to LDC combatants has declined. Budget reductions are expected in Saudi Arabia, and in Libya, where 1985 foreign reserves fell 20 percent from their 1984 level, economic cutbacks have already begun.[8] These developments suggest that the reliance of warring LDCs on the superpowers for military equipment and financial assistance, is likely to grow.

The dependency of the LDC combatants upon the superpowers in these areas is compounded by their need for and the superpowers' comparative strength in other equally vital services. Thus, although combatants may procure arms from many sources, few states other than the superpowers are able to produce or remove from their existing stores large quantities of major weapon systems without dangerously drawing down their own inventories. Fewer still have the capability to transport them rapidly over long distances along with men and support equipment. This is true for European as well as other LDC suppliers who do not have sufficient long-range air transports in inventory to carry heavy, outsize cargo to the theater of conflict (such as the U.S. C-5A, C-141, and C-130, or the Soviet An-22, or the An-400 currently in production).[9] When rapid transfers of troops or matériel have been necessary, the LDCs and countries in East and West Europe have had to turn to one of the superpowers for this type of equipment. France, for example, has been a relatively frequent user of large U.S. transports. In May 1978, during the second invasion of Zaire's Shaba province, the United States provided 18 C-141 transport aircraft for Belgian and French troops. And in 1984, during the French airlift of military supplies to Chad, the United States supplied a C-130 to facilitate deliveries.[10] Again, in 1986, the French chartered a U.S. transport, this time the Lockheed C-5 Galaxy, according to one source, because the payload – U.S.-built Hawk surface-to-air missiles – was too bulky to travel on French transports (including their large C-160 Transall).[11] Among Communist bloc states, it has been the USSR that supplies the logistics for the larger movements of Cuban troops and supplies.[12]

In addition to these comparative disadvantages, few suppliers, other than the superpowers, have enough global influence to negotiate permission for refueling or overflights from countries on the route of access. In those instances in which large scale emergency assistance is necessary, combatants have few options other than asking a superpower for assistance.

Finally, intelligence and satellite information, which provide real-time knowledge about enemy strength and movements, has become increasingly important to combat performance. Again, most states must rely on the United States or the Soviet Union for these services. The intelligence given to Great Britain by the United States during the Falklands war is one example, and the information gathered by U.S. tracking installations in Honduras and ground operators in the region that was provided to the Contras is another.[13] In both instances the assistance is credited with saving many lives. In the case of the Contras, U.S. data on the locations of the Sandinistas' fleet of helicopters is believed to have helped keep Contra casualties down in 1984. Much of the information was gathered at a U.S. radar station at Tiger Island in the Gulf of Fonseca and at a second radar station manned by the U.S. Air Force in the mountains near the Honduran capital, Tegucigalpa.[14] The Soviets, on the other hand, are rumored to have passed on some intelligence data to the Argentines, while diplomats report that Libya was without potentially helpful satellite material or other intelligence because the Soviet ships in the Mediterranean declined to provide them during the clashes between the Libyan forces and the U.S. Sixth Fleet in and around the Gulf of Sidra during March 1986.[15]

Ultimately, leverage in LDC wars rests with the superpowers, whose economic resources, which dwarf those of other states, enables them to dispense or refrain from supplying significant amounts and kinds of military aid. In this respect, even the Soviet Union is at a comparative disadvantage to the United States.

Economic slowdowns, beginning in the late 1970s, combined with low oil prices and declining production beginning in 1984, have compounded the Soviet Union's difficulties. In the first quarter of 1985, oil output contributing 60 percent of the Soviet hard currency earnings declined, leading to a $2 billion trade deficit in contrast to a surplus in the equivalent 1984 period.[16] In response to these problems, the USSR has come to rely more heavily on its arms export earnings and increasingly has been forced to demand hard currency payment for its weapon transfers. Whereas its 1950s agreements with LDCs were concessional with discounts ranging from 40–50 percent and easy financing terms, by 1981 an estimated 85 percent of the Soviet Union's arms sales were paid for in hard currency, and these sales were contributing 20 percent to the USSR's hard currency export earnings.[17]

In spite of these constraints, however, the Soviet Union remains a major economic power in the world, and when important political goals are at stake, it is capable and willing to provide generous military assistance on easy terms. Indian-Soviet relations provide a good illustration. They demonstrate not only the concessions the USSR is ready to make in certain situations, but also the degree to which the choices of recipients are circumscribed by financial constraints.

Heavily dependent upon the Soviet Union for military technology since 1971, the Indian government decided in the late 1970s to diversify its source of supply. But the Soviet's willingness to sell and permit the licensed production of some of their newer arms at concessional prices, their willingness to accept rupees in payment, plus India's chronic hard currency shortage, left the Indian government little choice. Although 116 new British Jaguar attack aircraft, another 40 French Mirage 2000 fighters, and 4 German submarines were ordered, India remains heavily dependent upon the Soviet Union as a source of supply.[18] In all probability, if the debts of the Third World continue to accumulate, more and more LDCs will, like India, be forced to turn to the superpowers for their military equipment and services. The pressures are even greater on countries waging expensive wars.

Constraints on Smaller and Middle Size Suppliers of Military Assistance

The above summary suggests that a subtle blend of LDC needs and the limited capabilities of other suppliers have enabled the superpowers to regulate the flow of major weapons to LDCs, particularly those fighting wars. This section examines more closely the relationship between the superpowers and smaller and middle size suppliers who are often accused of fanning the flames of conflict with their arms deliveries. It analyzes the assumption of some observers that a rise in the number of suppliers reduces the ability of the superpowers to regulate the arms trade, particularly during periods of crisis. It suggests that what may have been overlooked in this assumption is the source of initiative for resupply during recent wars. Have the multiple suppliers independently responded to the combatants' demand for resupply, or have they acted with the tacit approval or at the prompting of either the United States or the USSR? During combat, is diversification a product of market demand or superpower manipulation?

Although the evidence that exists is circumstantial, it points to considerable superpower control over military transfers regardless of source. In fact an argument can be made that much of the assistance received by belligerents from small and middle size donors can be classified as "indirect transfers" — that the increased diversification of supply during recent wars in many instances derives more from superpower political interests and influence than from the independent decisions of other donors and their Third World customers. The same may be true for military aid to LDCs in general.

The Influence of the Soviet Union

With regard to the relationship between the Soviet Union and
its allies and friends, the general literature on this question
is consensual. Analysts agree that military assistance programs are highly coordinated among Eastern bloc allies,
particularly between the Soviet Union and the East European socialist states, and that the structure of that coordination is hierarchical.[19] Through a system of third country
and indirect transfers, military aid from the Eastern bloc to
the LDCs in general and to combatants in particular has been
discreetly orchestrated by the Soviet Union. One source
points out that military transfers from Soviet allies to the
LDCs on behalf of the USSR are common, especially in instances where the latter does not wish to be "directly involved."[20] This was certainly the case at the onset of the Iran-
Iraq war, when the USSR was still temporizing over its
policy but continuing to resupply Iraq through other Warsaw
Pact countries while testing the waters in Iran. Although the
Soviet Union had officially embargoed arms sales to Iraq, the
German Democratic Republic (GDR), Poland, and Romania
continued to deliver T-54/55 tanks and other matériel to help
Iraq compensate for its vast losses. In Mozambique, another
area of conflict, Hungary furnished tanks and planes produced by the USSR or another Pact country (because Hungary produces neither itself), along with instructors and advisers to train Mozambique's military to use them.[21]

Even in instances when the Soviets do provide direct
military aid, most of the East European sales are appendages
to the larger Soviet program. One study concludes that "Soviet allies transfer arms to the third world only where this
suits Soviet purposes. . . . even when East European countries transfer arms to countries in the grey areas of Soviet
diplomacy, it is safe to assume that they act with the Krem-
lin's approval."[22]

A similar hierarchy of cooperation involves technical
assistance services and training. Here the division of labor
is thought to be quite defined. Some observers say Czecho-

slovakia specializes in training tank teams and artillery, the GDR in utilizing reconnaissance equipment and air traffic, Poland in training pilots and parachutists, and Hungary in the general training of infantry.[23] Others describe a somewhat different division of labor. One analyst notes:

> The Soviets provide most of the clout; the Cubans provide the necessary manpower; and the East Germans supply the highly sophisticated technical and administrative expertise so desperately needed in the emerging states.[24]

But whether the specifics of the division of labor among Eastern bloc states are correct or not, there is general agreement regarding the regulated character of Warsaw Pact military assistance programs. As one study concludes, "East German military advisors in Angola, Ethiopia, and Mozambique serve Soviet interests and are apparently supervised by Soviet personnel, as is surely the case for Cuban troops."[25] This conclusion regarding Soviet influence seems to apply in other recent wars when there have been no known cases of Eastern Europeans flouting Soviet transfer strictures.[26]

One important means of controlling the system has been Soviet reluctance to permit licensed production of modern major systems in neighboring countries, which might turn their weapons in the wrong direction or prove to be competitors in the arms market. After 1961, no East European country received new production licenses for any major Soviet weapon system, with the exception of tanks already in Soviet inventory for a number of years.[27] Today, among Warsaw Pact countries, no Soviet combat aircraft are manufactured outside the Soviet Union, and as far as is known, the T-64 and the new T-80 now in the Soviet inventory have not been issued to any other member of the Warsaw Pact, nor have they been exported.[28] The results have been an erosion of Eastern Europe's military-industrial capabilities, a decline in the competitiveness of their products in the world market, and relatively tight Soviet export control over their most advanced offensive technologies.

Less is known about the relationship between the Soviet Union and the military aid programs offered by its LDC friends and allies. Soviet policy has been equally restrictive regarding new coproduction and licensing agreements. Only India has been allowed to produce modern Soviet systems under license. But India has not been in a position to thwart Soviet political interests in this area, even if it so desired. A combination of production problems and a high demand from India's own military for its own defense industrial products has kept Indian arms exports very low.[29]

The relationship with Libya and North Korea, major purveyors of Soviet technologies, is more problematical. There have been reports that the size of North Korea's exports to Iran were troublesome to the Soviet Union and that in 1984 Moscow pressured Pyongyang to moderate them. One source contends that because of its economic and military dependency on the Soviet Union, North Korea enjoys little autonomy in these matters. The Soviets have driven a hard bargain for "second-rate, outdated" military equipment, and they have delayed and temporarily embargoed exports of contracted equipment, cutting off economic aid during some periods to express their displeasure with North Korean policies – with apparent success.[30]

The Libyan transfer of Scud B missiles to the Iranians also is said to have caused some friction between Col. Mu'ammar Qadhafi and the Soviets.[31] The delivery of four MiG-23s to North Korea in 1985 and the reported delay in Libya's then pending military aid package from the Soviet Union may not have been related to the compliance of the former and the transfer of the Soviet-made Scuds to Iran by the latter, but they may not be totally unrelated either.[32] In any event, these are only speculations, and there have been contrary rumors that the Soviets are simply keeping their options open in Iran with Libyan deliveries. What seems evident is that the exports of neither Libya nor North Korea have been able to change the relative balance in the Gulf. Even if there have been isolated infractions, in general, the military assistance offered by the Soviet Union's Third World allies and friends suggests as much support for Soviet policies as that given by the East Europeans.

The Influence of the United States

Although the connections are less clear in the West and U.S. friends are extremely sensitive to the charge of "surrogate" or "proxy," a similar hierarchical pattern of supply has emerged. Through a system of subtle persuasion, the prohibitions of transfers to third parties, and the promise of future economic or political rewards, as in the case of the Soviet Union the evidence suggests extensive U.S. influence over the flow of arms and services to combatants.

The complex indirect Western network supplying the Afghan rebels, discussed above, is only one example. Another is the struggle over the Western Sahara when, during the early days of the controversy, the United States turned to the shah's Iran to implement an intricate transfer of older U.S. aircraft and artillery to Morocco through Jordan.[33]

In Central America, the relationship is even clearer. Here the Reagan administration has publicly discussed the role of substitute suppliers. Thus, in the face of Congress's reluctance to support the Nicaraguan insurgents and as a tactic to persuade it to do so, the administration announced in March 1985 its intention to request friendly Asian countries to help channel aid to the Contras.[34] In August 1985, the Nicaraguan government claimed that South Korea had sent military experts to advise the Contras.[35] Other countries, heavily dependent upon the United States for economic and military support, such as Honduras, El Salvador, and Israel, have also reportedly increased their aid to the rebels substantially. Brazil, Venezuela, and Argentina are also said to be indirectly sending military equipment to the Contras. And Israel's role in the region has been referred to in the press as that of a "surrogate supplier."[36] Honduras, in exchange for allowing U.S. aid to the Contras to pass through its territory, has pressured successfully for increased U.S. military and economic aid.[37]

El Salvador has benefited from assistance proffered by an assortment of close U.S. allies, too. In addition to indirect equipment transfers, supplementary support has been forthcoming from European allies and Israel. Britain, Belgium, and Israel have each volunteered to train members of the Salvadoran army in their countries, and West Germany lifted a five-year ban on aid to El Salvador in 1984 by providing technical and financial assistance.[38]

On the other hand, U.S. efforts to limit Nicaragua's access to Western equipment have also been quite effective, despite the disinclination of U.S. friends to honor them. France, however reluctantly, acquiesced to the Reagan administration's request that it "slow down" delivery of an arms package it had sold to the Sandinista regime in Nicaragua. The French also agreed to "delay" delivery of the two Alouette III helicopters the United States found most objectionable. Senior U.S. officials reportedly said they thought any new French arms deals with Nicaragua "most unlikely."[39] Other European and Latin American countries have followed suit, so that Nicaragua, once the recipient of military assistance from multiple Western suppliers, now finds itself almost completely dependent upon Communist bloc states for military aid.

The widespread and successful U.S. effort to isolate Nicaragua is demonstrated by U.S.-Mexican exchanges on this issue. According to one source, in 1984 Mexico was backing away from its strong support of the Nicaraguan Sandinista government and the rebels in El Salvador, in deference to President Reagan's request that it do so. It halted all shipments of oil to Nicaragua (in part because of Nicaragua's backlog of overdue payments), began pressuring guerrillas living in Mexico to end their public activities, and stopped endorsing the Salvadoran guerrillas. Professor George Dominguez is quoted as saying that "Mexican leaders also felt they were getting too close to a break with Washington over Central America and wanted to head off pressures, particularly given the precarious state of the Mexican economy."[40]

The Horn war provides further examples. Although the United States refused to transfer weapons to Somalia, persistent rumors circulated in the U.S. press that the United States had permitted Saudi Arabia to purchase new U.S. weapons for Egypt in exchange for the delivery of Egypt's older Soviet-built weapons to Somalia.[41] Ethiopia also accused the United States of secretly collaborating with Iran, Saudi Arabia, and Egypt to supply Somalia with other arms purchased in Western Europe and the United States and sent from West Germany and Iran. Since the war's end, Egypt has continued to help train Somali troops for their skirmishes against Ethiopia, and it is supplying them with armored vehicles, antitank rockets, and other weapons and ammunition.[42]

The Combined Influence of the Superpowers

The examples above offer some evidence of the influence the superpowers individually have exercised over the flow of arms and services to combatants in recent wars. The extent of superpower control, however, is perhaps least elusive in and best illustrated by the Iran-Iraq war. Both superpowers have evinced intense interest in the war, monitoring it closely, the United States with U.S.-manned airborne warning and control system (AWACS) aircraft on loan to Saudi Arabia, the Soviets by satellite.[43] Because they share the goal of containing violence in the Middle East, the United States and the USSR have moved to limit the flow of sophisticated weapons to both combatants.

On the Soviet side, although the USSR has provided the bulk of Iraq's arms since the spring of 1982, it has refrained from delivering systems that might upset the Middle East balance or the Gulf stalemate. Its relations with Iran have been equally careful. The Soviets have not supplied modern major weapons, and apparently they have successfully prevailed upon North Korea to keep their exports to Iran moderate[44]. To date, North Korean transfers have consisted of older, less advanced systems and large quantities of ammunition and quartermaster supplies – items Iran needs to carry on the war, but no major weapons that might upset the balance. Warsaw Pact states have also been restrained by the Soviets from sending larger items to Iran.

Until late 1983, the United States maintained a generally neutral posture on the Gulf war, refusing to assist either side with military goods. During the first two years of the war, while Iran was on the defensive, the United States ignored, some say "allowed," third party sales of U.S.-made parts and munitions to Iran.[45] But when the tide seemed to be turning in Iran's favor, a secret U.S. National Security Decision Directive was issued in November 1983, which led to a series of actions often described as a "tilt" toward Iraq. As one State Department official expressed it, "We want to keep Iraq in the field and get the war ended."[46] Since then, the United States has provided some financial and other purportedly nonmilitary aid to Iraq, offered air protection to other Arab states against Iranian attacks on shipping, pressured Western and Asian nations to reduce their arms supplies to Iran, and encouraged moderate assistance to Iraq.

U.S. pressure on its allies regarding assistance to Iran has been discreet but not unsuccessful. The Europeans have agreed to stop deliveries to Iran, with the exception of prior, prerevolution orders, and although there is still a lively black market in spares, small arms, and ammunition, since mid-1983, even this, according to U.S. State Department officials, has slowed as U.S. containment efforts have become more focused.[47]

America's LDC allies have also cooperated, although often reluctantly. South Korea reportedly has refrained from further shipments to Iran since mid-1984, and in late 1984 or early 1985 Israel revised its arms sales policy to the Gulf, stopping all military shipments to Iran as well.[48] As a result of pressure from the United States, China, too, apparently stopped transiting arms to Iran through North Korea in mid-

1984 and broke off a proposed $1 billion sale of fighters and tanks to the government of Ayatollah Khomeini.[49] And in June 1984 the Brazilians banned arms sales to Iran. Brazil reportedly agreed to restrict its weapons sales abroad "in return for access to U.S. defence technology."[50] As a result, Iran has been unable to acquire any modern major weapons since the beginning of the war.

Because the Iran-Iraq war is the most lucrative market in the Third World and because most producing countries, European as well as LDCs, badly need the foreign exchange to support their own military industries and U.S. procurements, acquiescence to U.S. pressure represents a significant sacrifice and demonstrates the weight of the United States in the arms trade system. South Korea's economic incentive to export to the Gulf states, for example, derives at least in part from Seoul's partially idle defense industries, which are running at one-third to one-half capacity. Similar motives drive European companies. According to press reports, an Austrian firm, Voest-Alpine, was sustaining heavy losses and had been trying to recoup them through "back-door" illegal arms sales to Iran when caught in the act. France, too, is considered export-dependent in the military sector and has often resisted U.S. attempts to limit its sales to warring Third World countries.[51] Given the domestic pull for arms transfers among U.S. friends and allies, the relative success of the U.S.-inspired embargo on Iran is all the more telling.

Supplies to Iraq from Western sources have also been sensitive to U.S. interests. One analyst claims that the United States in mid-1982, concerned about a possible Iranian breakthrough but officially still neutral toward both Gulf belligerents, relied primarily upon France to prevent Iraq's collapse. Increased deliveries of French weapons began arriving in 1983 and 1984, which may have served as a partial offset for their cooperation vis-à-vis Iran. It is noteworthy, however, that despite the increases in quality and quantity of French arms transferred to Iraq, they have not been sufficient to give Baghdad a decisive advantage, a testament, according to some observers, to both Iraq's unimpressive use of French equipment in combat and the relative export restraint of the French.[52]

Thus, although there are still weaknesses in the system, when the political stakes are high and the superpowers are united, they have been able to slow the flow and contain the level of sophistication of equipment entering the region of combat. Their methods for doing so are not dissimilar.

As we have seen, control over the diffusion of major weapon systems is possible for the Soviet Union because it limits licensed production abroad and serves as sole supplier to Eastern Europe. Corroborating the evidence presented above, one State Department official observed, "The Warsaw Pact states are so dependent upon the U.S.S.R. for spares for their own military equipment and for new technologies, the Soviets have them over a barrel in situations like this."[53] Ultimately, in Eastern Europe, as another commentator notes, Soviet control is supported "by force of Soviet arms."[54]

For the United States, third party transfer prohibitions have been a potent U.S. weapon.[55] Because many of the advanced major systems in Western inventories are U.S.-made and because a large number of the sophisticated subsystems contained in the domestically produced items of U.S. allies are supplied by the United States, the United States, through agreements prohibiting retransfer, is able to regulate their spread to third parties. These restrictions have worked well in the past and apparently have been used with equal success during recent wars.[56] Even after the armed hostilities over the Falklands had ended, the United States blocked Israel's sale of aging A-4 Skyhawk aircraft to Argentina based on its right as original seller to prohibit sales to third parties.[57]

Because the development of advanced military technology requires a large research and development (R&D) effort, which only the United States and USSR have been able to afford, most states remain dependent upon the superpowers for their most advanced systems and components. Although estimates of Soviet R&D expenditures are not readily available, one source suggests a range within one-third and two-fifths of the world total. In 1983, of the estimated $60 billion world expenditure on military R&D, the superpowers' share was thought to be about four-fifths (or $48 billion).[58]

Estimates are that the United States spends three to four times more than Europe on conventional military R&D, which has meant that individual European countries have had to rely on U.S. R&D efforts not only for advanced major systems but also for the sophisticated subsystems incorporated into their own indigenously produced items. For example, 30 percent of each Tornado plane produced jointly by the UK, West Germany, and Italy reflects imported U.S. equipment.[59] Soviet allies find themselves in a similar position. Clearly, continued access to modern technology has been an important incentive for many countries, developed and less developed, to accept and adhere to U.S. and Soviet third country transfer restraints.

In addition, the superpowers are able to use economic assistance and the promise of future military sales to obtain cooperation. The financial needs of most states has made this, perhaps, the most powerful leverage of all. In return, many are willing, even eager, to perform various military assistance services. Thus, the $3.2 billion U.S. aid package to Pakistan is said to be, in part, compensation for Pakistan's support of the Afghan insurgency. Moreover, some observers believe Israel's enlarged economic and military assistance from the United States is related to Israeli activities in Central America.[60] In some instances, a military sale to a combatant by a U.S. ally also may have been a tacit offset to its own U.S. procurements. Although this kind of relationship is difficult to document, and for obvious reasons rarely discussed openly by either party, the precedent is not unknown. In the 1960s the British sold $266 million worth of Lightning aircraft, missiles, a radar system, and training services to Saudi Arabia, in spite of Saudia Arabia's declared preference for a U.S. plane. They did so with the direct encouragement of President John F. Kennedy's administration, "which understood that Britain would use the money from the sale to purchase U.S.-manufactured fighter aircraft."[61] At issue was the British balance of payments problems and their prospective purchase of U.S. F-111 aircraft. According to one source, the Saudis "had been persuaded to buy British planes that they did not want, to allow Britain to pay for American planes it could not afford."[62]

In a different context, Britain again served as a substitute supplier for the United States when it sold $4 billion worth of fighter planes (72 Tornado jet fighters, 30 Swiss PC-9 trainers that British Aerospace Public Limited Co. [BAe] is modifying to Saudi requirements, and 30 Hawk trainers) to Saudi Arabia in lieu of two squadrons of the U.S. F-15 aircraft. Unwilling or unable to pay the political price necessary to get the F-15 package through Congress, in mid-summer 1985 the Reagan administration sent a letter to the Saudis "that raised no objections to purchases of planes elsewhere."[63] And as one English informant observed, "We couldn't say that Reagan steered the Saudis in Britain's direction. We like to think, and Mrs. Thatcher likes to think, that we all have a close relationship. Certainly in a political sense, this government, Reagan and the Saudis are all very close."[64] Although no documentation exists establishing a direct connection between the military aid activities of U.S. (or Soviet) allies and friends and offsets for their procurements, based on the few cases that have surfaced it is not illogical to assume a connection in some situations. More apparent is the relationship between increased economic aid and surrogate activities.

Hence, the dependence of most states, European as well as LDCs, upon one or the other of the superpowers for sophisticated military technologies, subsystems, advanced R&D, and other forms of economic and military support has been a powerful incentive for cooperation and compliance. Through a delicate system of tacit rewards for restraint and punishment for infractions, both superpowers have been able to "staunch the flow" and regulate the level of armed hostilities in various regions of the world.

This discussion has not meant to suggest that superpower control has been or can be total. The participating countries have reasons of their own for cooperating and often pursue their own political and economic interests even when they promote those of one of the superpowers. And when the basic interests of a superpower's allies or friends are at stake, they may not be compliant. Still, the United States and the USSR retain the option of withdrawing support and wreaking economic punishment if sufficiently displeased — a price most smaller or less affluent states are frequently unwilling to bear.

In sum, a constellation of factors has served to foster the dependency of most of the world's states on the economic and technological capabilities of the superpowers. As a result, the intensity of combat in the Third World has been determined not only by the regional interests of the combatants but by the national interests of the United States and USSR as well.

Judging from recent conflicts in the Third World, neither war nor the rising number of weapon suppliers have served to destabilize the international system or reduce the influence of the United States and USSR in it. To date, the superpowers have not clashed with each other on the battlefield, and their military competition has been relegated to direct and indirect support of combatants in local wars. Both have continued to dominate the arms trade, using military assistance both to enhance their position in the world and to limit each other's expansion.

Although diversification and indirect sources of supply have permitted Third World combatants to continue fighting, often at tremendous cost in lives, the type of weapons and training available to them has remained limited. In effect, the superpowers have retained control over the quality if not the quantity of the arms trade, and ultimately, therefore, over the level of technological sophistication at which wars can be fought in the Third World.

APPENDIX 1
Military Assistance to Third World Combatants (through 1983)
Averaged $ Value (millions) and % of Total Value (deliveries)

	Prewar[1]													
	Eastern Europe		USSR		Western Europe[6]		United States		Third World		Other Significant Supplier		Total SP	
	$	%	$	%	$	%	$	%	$	%	$	%	$	
Ethiopia	1.8	3.9	0.06	0.1	5.5	11.9	22.9	49.4	16.1	34.7	–	–	46.4	DM**
Somalia	0.1	0.1	79.5	98.6	1.0	1.2	–	–	–	–	–	–	80.6	M†
Afghanistan[4]	–	–	27.9	98.6	0.03	0.1	0.2	0.7	0.2	0.7	–	–	28.3	M†
Morocco	–	–	2.0	1.0	159.3	76.9	38.5	18.6	7.4	3.6	(FR	42.5)	207.2	DM**
Nicaragua	–	–	–	–	2.1	24.7	2.6	30.6	3.8	44.7	(IS	36.0)	8.5	DM**
Honduras	0.8	5.2	–	–	0.5	3.2	3.2	20.6	11.0	71.0	(IS	66.5)	15.5	P**
El Salvador	–	–	–	–	0.1	2.9	1.8	51.4	1.6	45.7	(IS	45.7)	3.5	DM**
Vietnam[5]	4.1	10.1	36.3	89.6	0.1	0.2	–	–	–	–	–	–	40.5	M†
PRC[5]	–	–	31.4	27.9	77.1	68.5	0.3	0.3	3.7	3.3	(UK	58.0)	112.5	I/P**

(continued)

APPENDIX 1
(Continued)

	Prewar[1]													
	Eastern Europe		USSR		Western Europe[6]		United States		Third World		Other Significant Supplier		Total SP	
	$	%	$	%	$	%	$	%	$	%	$	%	$	
Iran	0.2	—	258.0	12.7	187.1	9.2	1530.1	75.4	54.5	2.7	—	—	2029.9	P*
Iraq	254.1	13.7	1209.2	65.4	357.9	19.4	0.03	—	28.4	1.5	—	—	1849.6	P†
Argentina	—	—	—	—	281.0	75.2	23.3	6.2	69.3	18.5	—	—	373.6	I/DM**
Syria[7]	127.2	5.8	1893.6	85.9	153.6	7.0	0.07	—	28.7	1.3	—	—	2203.2	P†
Israel	—	—	—	—	1.5	0.2	883.5	99.8	—	—	—	—	885.0	I/M*
$ Total	388.3		3538.0		1226.8		2506.5		224.7		—		7884.3	
% Total		4.9		44.8		15.6		31.8		2.8		—		

Source: Derived from U.S. government sources.

128

DM–Diversified or Multiple suppliers: two suppliers each with 45%+ of the market, or 3+ suppliers none of which provides more than 49% of a recipient's military assistance.

I–Indigenous production capability for major weapons.

M–Monopoly: one supplier provides 90%+ of all military assistance.

P–Principal supplier: one supplier provides 50%–89%.

SP–Supply pattern.

EG–Egypt; FR–France; GDR–German Democratic Republic (East Germany); IS–Israel; IT–Italy; NK–North Korea; PR–Peru; UK–United Kingdom.

*–U.S.; **–Western Bloc; †–USSR; ††–Eastern Bloc.

1 – *Prewar Period*: 2–3 years prior to onset of war; Dollar value averaged.

2 – *War Period*: Up to and including 1983 (estimate for 1983 only); Dollar value averaged.

3 – *Postwar Period*: Years after the cessation of hostilities, up to and including 1983 (estimate for 1983 only); Dollar value averaged. Prewar years 1954–1977 dollar value averaged.

4 – War years for Afghanistan calculated from 1978–1982; Dollar value averaged; Prewar years 1954–1977 dollar value averaged.

5 – Postwar years up to and including 1982.

6 – Canada, Japan, and Australia included (represent small amount of total).

7 – Total dollar value of Soviet resupply for Syria in 1983 not included.

129

(*continued*)

APPENDIX 1
(Continued)

	Eastern Europe		USSR		Western Europe[6]		War[2] United States		Third World		Other Significant Supplier		Total SP	
	$	%	$	%	$	%	$	%	$	%	$	%	$	
Ethiopia	41.0	5.4	650.0	84.9	15.3	2.0	35.3	4.6	24.1	3.1	–	–	765.7	P†
Somalia	2.0	1.3	26.0	17.0	61.6	40.3	–	–	63.2	41.4	(EG 29.0)	(IT 24.0)	152.8	DM
Afghanistan[4]	1.5	1.1	130.8	98.7	–	–	0.2	0.2	–	–	–	–	132.5	M†
Morocco	2.8	0.8	0.3	0.1	247.9	69.1	91.4	25.5	16.4	4.6	(FR	52.8)	358.8	P**

	$	%	$	%	$	%	$	%	$	%		Total	
Nicaragua	1.4	24.6	25.8	55.6	1.9	4.1	0.02	—	7.3	15.7	(GDR 17.0)	46.4	P†
Honduras	—	—	—	—	1.6	20.8	5.1	66.2	1.0	13.0	—	7.7	P*
El Salvador	—	—	—	—	5.5	18.3	24.1	80.1	0.5	1.7	—	30.1	P*
Vietnam[5]	—	—	—	—	—	—	—	—	—	—	—	—	—
PRC[5]	—	—	—	—	—	—	—	—	—	—	—	—	—
Iran	22.0	2.8	74.8	9.5	191.4	24.4	—	—	496.0	63.2	(NK 29.0)	784.2	DM
Iraq	652.8	19.8	1091.6	33.2	961.2	29.2	—	—	586.2	17.8	—	3291.8	DM
Argentina	11.1	11.1	—	—	27.7	27.6	—	—	61.4	61.2	(PR 60.4)	100.2	I/P**
Syria[7]	—	—	—	—	—	—	—	—	—	—	—	—	—
Israel	—	—	—	—	—	—	—	—	—	—	—	—	—
$ Total	734.6		1999.3		1514.1		156.1		1256.1			5660.2	
% Total		12.9		35.3		26.7		2.8		22.2			

(continued)

APPENDIX 1
(Continued)

						Postwar[3]							
	Eastern Europe		USSR		Western Europe[6]		United States		Third World		Other Significant Supplier		Total SP
	$	%	$	%	$	%	$	%	$	%	$	%	$
Ethiopia	7.8	2.7	266.0	93.0	6.2	2.2	–	–	6.0	2.1	–	–	286.0 M†
Somalia	2.4	2.3	–	–	78.0	73.8	7.7	7.3	17.6	16.7	(IT	70.0)	105.7 P**
Afghanistan[4]	–	–	–	–	–	–	–	–	–	–	–	–	–
Morocco	–	–	–	–	–	–	–	–	–	–	–	–	–

Country	$	%	$	%	$	%	$	%	$	%		Total	
Nicaragua	—	—	—	—	—	—	—	—	—	—	—	—	—
Honduras	—	—	—	—	—	—	—	—	—	—	—	—	—
El Salvador	—	—	—	—	—	—	—	—	—	—	—	—	—
Vietnam[5]	0.8	0.1	690.4	99.9	—	—	0.2	—	—	—	—	691.4	M†
PRC[5]	—	—	32.8	26.9	88.3	72.7	0.4	0.3	—	—	(UK 43.0)	121.5	I/DM
Iran	—	—	—	—	—	—	—	—	—	—	—	—	—
Iraq	—	—	—	—	—	—	—	—	—	—	—	—	—
Argentina	—	—	—	—	652.6	78.4	16.3	2.0	162.7	19.6	(FRG 65.0)	831.6	P**
Syria[7]	110.0	7.2	1200.0	78.9	166.7	11.0	—	—	44.5	2.9	—	1521.2	P†
Israel	—	—	—	—	—	—	790.4	100.0	—	—	—	790.4	I/M*
$ Total	121.0		2189.2		992.0		814.8		230.8			4347.8	
% Total	2.8		50.4		22.8		18.7		5.3				

APPENDIX 2
Comparative Force Structures: Design Origin of Weapon Systems in Inventory and Percent of Total[1]

Origin[2]	Recipients	Combat Aircraft								Helicopters							
		1976–77		1977–78		1978–79		1979–80		1976–77		1977–78		1978–79		1979–80	
		Total	%	Total	%	Total	%	Total	%	Total	%	Total	%	Total	%	Total	%
	Ethiopia																
United States		32	88.8	33	94.2	27	27.2	13	13.0	6	37.5	10	37.0	10	17.8	10	20.4
USSR		–	–	–	–	70	70.7	87	87.0	–	–	2	7.4	30	53.5	25	51.0
Britain		4	11.1	2	5.7	2	2.0	–	–	–	–	–	–	–	–	–	–
France		–	–	–	–	–	–	–	–	–	–	5	18.5	6	10.7	4	8.1
Italy		–	–	–	–	–	–	–	–	10	62.5	10	37.0	10	17.8	10	20.4
	Somalia																
United States		–	–	–	–	–	–	–	–	–	–	–	–	–	–	–	–
USSR		66	100.0	55	100.0	25	100.0	22	100.0	16	100.0	10	90.9	10	90.9	10	90.9
Italy		–	–	–	–	–	–	–	–	–	–	1	9.0	1	9.0	1	9.0

	1979–80		1980–81		1981–82		1982–83		1979–80		1980–81		1981–82		1982–83	
Iran																
United States	447	100.0	451	100.0	349	100.0	90	100.0	749	85.6	643	84.0	620	88.0	599	89.0
USSR	—	—	—	—	—	—	—	—	—	—	—	—	—	—	—	—
Britain	—	—	—	—	—	—	—	—	—	—	—	—	—	—	—	—
France	—	—	—	—	—	—	—	—	16	1.8	16	2.0	16	2.0	—	—
Italy	—	—	—	—	—	—	—	—	109	12.4	109	14.0	72	10.0	72	11.0
Iraq																
United States	—	—	—	—	—	—	—	—	—	—	—	—	—	—	—	—
USSR	319	94.0	317	95.0	287	86.0	287	86.0	129	56.0	169	61.0	238	65.0	241	64.0
Britain	20	6.0	15	5.0	12	4.0	12	4.0	40	17.0	47	17.0	57	16.0	63	17.0
France	—	—	—	—	36	11.0	36	11.0	62	27.0	60	22.0	71	19.0	71	19.0
Czechoslovakia	—	—	—	—	—	—	—	—	—	—	—	—	—	—	—	—
Switzerland	—	—	—	—	—	—	—	—	—	—	—	—	—	—	—	—
Hungary	—	—	—	—	—	—	—	—	—	—	—	—	—	—	—	—
Brazil	—	—	—	—	—	—	—	—	—	—	—	—	—	—	—	—

[1]Derived from *The Military Balance, 1976/77–1983/84* (London: The International Institute for Strategic Studies).

[2]Data does not include local production. Imports only.

(continued)

APPENDIX 2
(Continued)

136

		Tanks								Armored Personnel Carriers							
		1976-77		1977-78		1978-79		1979-80		1976-77		1977-78		1978-79		1979-80	
Origin	Recipients	Total	%	Total	%	Total	%	Total	%	Total	%	Total	%	Total	%	Total	%
	Ethiopia																
United States		78	100.0	105	75.0	54	9.0	80	11.7	90	100.0	90	69.2	70	18.9	70	12.0
USSR		—	—	35	25.0	500	90.9	600	88.2	—	—	40	30.7	300	81.0	512	87.9
Britain		—	—	—	—	—	—	—	—	—	—	—	—	—	—	—	—
France		—	—	—	—	—	—	—	—	—	—	—	—	—	—	—	—
Italy		—	—	—	—	—	—	—	—	—	—	—	—	—	—	—	—
	Somalia																
United States		—	—	—	—	—	—	—	—	—	—	—	—	—	—	—	—
USSR		250	100.0	300	100.0	80	100.0	80	100.0	310	100.0	350	100.0	150	100.0	150	100.0
Italy		—	—	—	—	—	—	—	—	—	—	—	—	—	—	—	—

	1979–80	1980–81	1981–82	1982–83	1979–80	1980–81	1981–82	1982–83
Iran								
United States	860 43.0	860 43.0	790 48.0	500 41.0	325 39.0	325 39.0	240 38.0	220 38.0
USSR	1125 57.0	1125 57.0	840 52.0	190 16.0	500 61.0	500 61.0	400 62.0	360 62.0
Britain	—	—	—	520 43.0	—	—	—	—
France	—	—	—	—	—	—	—	—
Italy	—	—	—	—	—	—	—	—
Iraq								
United States	—	—	—	—	—	—	—	—
USSR	1900 100.0	2750 96.0	2600 96.0	2300 100.0	500*	833* 33.0	333* 17.0	560* 17.0
Britain	—	—	—	—	—	—	—	—
France	—	100 4.0	100 4.0	—	500*	833* 33.0	333* 17.0	560* 17.0
Czechoslovakia	—	—	—	—	500*	833* 33.0	333* 17.0	560* 17.0
Switzerland	—	—	—	—	—	—	333* 17.0	560* 17.0
Hungary	—	—	—	—	—	—	333* 17.0	560* 17.0
Brazil	—	—	—	—	—	—	333* 17.0	200* 17.0

*No country breakdown figures are given for APC transfers in 1979–1983. These figures are arrived at by dividing total number of APCs equally among donor countries; hence, the possibility of deflated/inflated figures for any one specific supplier.

(continued)

APPENDIX 2
(Continued)

Argentina

Origin	Combat Aircraft 1979-80 Total	%	1980-81 Total	%	1981-82 Total	%	Helicopters 1979-80 Total	%	1980-81 Total	%	1981-82 Total	%
United States	95	49.0	91	43.0	81	48.0	103	75.5	80	66.0	102	64.0
Britain	9	4.0	9	4.0	9	5.0	3	2.0	3	2.0	3	2.0
France	91	47.0	110	52.0	79	47.0	32	23.0	30	25.0	48	27.0
Sweden	—		—		—		—		—		—	
Federal Republic of Germany	—		—		—		—		—		—	
Italy	—		—		—		—		9	7.0	9	6.0
Belgium	—		—		—		—		—		—	

Israel[3]

Origin	Combat Aircraft 1980-81 Total	%	1981-82 Total	%	1982-83 Total	%	Helicopters 1980-81 Total	%	1981-82 Total	%	1982-83 Total	%
United States	355	92.0	462	94.5	426	95.5	121	80.0	143	94.0	179	96.0
France	30	8.0	27	5.5	20	4.5	30	20.0	10	6.0	8	4.0
Britain	—		—		—		—		—		—	
Egypt	—		—		—		—		—		—	

Syria

Origin	Combat Aircraft 1980-81 Total	%	1981-82 Total	%	1982-83 Total	%	Helicopters 1980-81 Total	%	1981-82 Total	%	1982-83 Total	%
USSR	395	100.0	446	100.0	450	100.0	90	72.0	106	73.0	101	67.0
Britain	—		—		—		35	28.0	40	27.0	49	33.0
Czechoslovakia	—		—		—		—		—		—	

[3]Israel had 80 Kfirs in inventory in 1980–1981; 85 in 1981–1982; 160 in 1982–1983.

Tanks and Armored Personnel Carriers

Argentina

Origin	Tanks 1979–80 Total	%	1980–81 Total	%	1981–82 Total	%	APC 1979–80 Total	%	1980–81 Total	%	1981–82 Total	%
United States	100	45.5	100	31.0	60	18.0	325	47.4	325	47.4	325	47.7
Britain	–	–	–	–	–	–	–	–	–	–	–	–
France	120	54.5	120	38.0	120	40.0	300	43.8	300	43.8	300	44.1
Sweden	–	–	–	–	–	–	60	8.9	60	8.9	50	7.4
Federal Republic of Germany	–	–	100	31.0	125	41.0	–	–	–	–	–	–
Italy	–	–	–	–	–	–	–	–	–	–	–	–
Belgium	–	–	–	–	–	–	–	–	–	–	5	0.7

Israel

Origin	Tanks 1980–81 Total	%	1981–82 Total	%	1982–83 Total	%	APC 1980–81 Total	%	1981–82 Total	%	1982–83 Total	%
United States	1460	46.0	1460	49.3	1668	52.7	***		***		***	
France	–	–	–	–	–	–	–	–	–	–	–	–
Britain	1000	32.0	1100	37.2	1100	34.7	***		***		***	
Egypt**	615	20.0	400	13.5	400	12.6						

Syria

Origin	Tanks 1980–81 Total	%	1981–82 Total	%	1982–83 Total	%	APC 1980–81 Total	%	1981–82 Total	%	1982–83 Total	%
USSR	2380	100.0	3700	100.0	3990	100.0	800	50.0	800	50.0	800	50.0
France	–	–	–	–	–	–	–	–	–	–	–	–
Britain	–	–	–	–	–	–	–	–	–	–	–	–
Czechoslovakia	–	–	–	–	–	–	800	50.0	800	50.0	800	50.0

(continued)

**Soviet origin captured weapons.
***About 4,000 APCs in inventory. Unknown breakdown.

139

APPENDIX 2
(Continued)

Origin	Combat Aircraft								Helicopters							
	1978-79		1979-80		1980-81		1981-82		1978-79		1979-80		1980-81		1981-82	
Recipients	Total	%	Total	%	Total	%	Total	%	Total	%	Total	%	Total	%	Total	%
Vietnam																
United States	–	–	105†	21.0	85††	18.0	85	18.0	–	–	120†	55.0	120†	55.0	90†	55.0
USSR	300	100.0	390	79.0	390	82.0	400	82.0	39	100.0	100	45.0	90	45.0	75	45.0
People's Republic of China	–		–		–		–		–		–		–		–	
Morocco																
United States	39	100.0	25	50.0	18	26.0	15	35.0	6	7.0	10	9.0	14	12.0	15	13.0
USSR	–		–		–		–		–		–		–		–	
Britain	–		–		–		–		–		3	3.0	3	3.0	3	3.0
France	–		25	50.0	50	74.0	28	65.0	40	44.0	44	41.0	44	37.0	37	33.0
Italy	–		–		–		–		44	49.0	50	47.0	59	49.0	58	51.0
Czechoslovakia	–		–		–		–		–		–		–		–	
Federal Republic of Germany	–		–		–		–		–		–		–		–	

	1979–80		1980–81		1981–82		1982–83	
Honduras								
United States	12	67.0	12	50.0	12	50.0	10	45.0
France	6	33.0	12	50.0	12	50.0	12	55.0
Britain	—		—		—		—	
Nicaragua								
United States	11	100.0	11	100.0	10	100.0	8	100.0
USSR	—		—		—		—	
El Salvador								
United States	25	100.0	—		—		—	
France	—		31	100.0	—		23	100.0
Federal Republic of Germany	—		—		25	100.0	—	

	1979–80		1980–81		1981–82		1982–83	
Honduras								
United States	2	67.0	2	67.0	—		12	100.0
France	1	33.0	1	33.0	—		—	
Britain	—		—		—		—	
Nicaragua								
United States	8	100.0	8	100.0	7	100.0	2	50.0
USSR	—		—		—		2	50.0
El Salvador								
United States	1	20.0	1	20.0	11	85.0	16	88.0
France	4	80.0	4	80.0	2	15.0	2	12.0
Federal Republic of Germany	—		—		—		—	

†U.S. aircraft probably captured in 1975.

††Note the change in U.S. aircraft: 10 F-5A and 10 F-37B are no longer in inventory in 1980–1981.

(continued)

APPENDIX 2
(Continued)

Origin	Recipients	Tanks 1978–79 Total	%	1979–80 Total	%	1980–81 Total	%	1981–82 Total	%	Armored Personnel Carriers 1978–79 Total	%	1979–80 Total	%	1980–81 Total	%	1981–82 Total	%
	Vietnam																
United States		–	–	550	27.5	550	22.0	550	22.0	–	–	800	7.4	800	35.0	800	35.0
USSR		900	100.0	950	47.0	1725	69.0	1725	69.0	†††	100.0	1000	9.3	1500	65.0	1500	65.0
People's Republic of China		–	–	500	25.0	225	9.0	225	9.0	–	–	–	–	–	–	–	–
	Morocco																
United States		130	76.0	180	82.0	230	88.0	230	88.0	140	61.0	370	80.0	404	54.0	404	54.0
USSR		40	24.0	40	18.0	30	12.0	30	12.0	–	–	–	–	240	32.0	240	32.0
Britain		–	–	–	–	–	–	–	–	–	–	–	–	–	–	–	–
France		–	–	–	–	–	–	–	–	–	–	–	–	–	–	–	–
Italy		–	–	–	–	–	–	–	–	–	–	–	–	–	–	–	–

	1979–80		1980–81		1981–82		1982–83		1979–80		1980–81		1981–82		1982–83	
Honduras																
Czechoslovakia	60	26.0	60	13.0	70	9.0	70	9.0	—	—	—	—	—	—	—	—
Federal Republic of Germany	30	13.0	30	7.0	30	4.0	30	4.0	—	—	—	—	—	—	—	—
United States	—	—	—	—	—	—	—	—	—	—	—	—	—	—	—	—
France	—	—	—	—	—	—	—	—	—	—	—	—	—	—	—	—
Britain	—	—	—	—	—	—	—	—	—	—	—	—	17	100.0	17	100.0
Nicaragua																
United States	—	—	—	—	—	—	—	—	?	100.0	2	100.0	3	50.0	3	11.0
USSR	—	—	—	—	—	—	—	—	—	—	—	—	3	50.0	25	89.0
El Salvador																
United States	—	—	—	—	—	—	—	—	12	100.0	12	100.0	12	100.0	12	100.0
France	—	—	—	—	—	—	—	—	—	—	—	—	—	—	—	—
Federal Republic of Germany	—	—	—	—	—	—	—	—	—	—	—	—	—	—	—	—

†††Unknown number of APCs.

Notes

Chapter 1

1. Although power has proved to be a difficult concept to define and measure, the field of international relations has come to associate it with the ability of one actor to influence the behavior of another. See Hans Morgenthau, *Power Among Nations*, 4th ed. (New York: Alfred A. Knopf, 1967), 9; Robert O. Keohane and Joseph S. Nye, Jr., *Power and Interdependence: World Politics in Transition* (Boston, Mass.: Little, Brown, 1977), 11.

2. The term loss of control is used by Nye and Keohane to refer to the relative inability of states to control policy outcomes. See Joseph S. Nye, Jr. and Robert O. Keohane, "Transnational Relations and World Politics: An Introduction," *Transnational Relations and World Politics*, Keohane and Nye, eds. (Cambridge, Mass.: Harvard University Press, 1972), xxiii.

3. U.S. Arms Control and Disarmanent Agency (ACDA), "Third World Arms Production," *World Military Expenditures and Arms Transfers, 1969-1978* (Washington, D.C.: ACDA, December 1980), 21.

4. Andrew J. Pierre, *The Global Politics of Arms Sales* (Princeton, N.J.: Princeton University Press, 1982), 4.

5. The following framework owes much to earlier work by Amelia Leiss, et al., *Arms Transfers to Less Developed Countries* (Cambridge, Mass.: Center for International Studies, Massachusetts Institute of Technology, 1970). Ronald Slaughter, "The Poli-

tics and Nature of the Conventional Arms Transfer Process during a Military Engagement: The Falklands-Malvinas Case," *Arms Control* (May 1983), 16–30 has also contributed a useful typology of arms supply relationships.

6. The five types of arms supply relationships are monopoly, monopolistic competition, duopoly, oligopoly, and free market. See Leiss, et al., *Arms Transfers*, 54 and 97.

7. ACDA, *World Military Expenditures and Arms Transfers, 1972–1982* (Washington, D.C.: ACDA, April 1984), 106.

8. Author interview with U.S. State Department analyst, January 1984.

Chapter 2

1. Leiss, et al., *Arms Transfers*, 97.

2. For a more detailed comparison and breakdown of the structure of the arms trade, see Stephanie G. Neuman, "The Arms Trade and U.S. National Interests," *Power and Policy in Transition*, Vojtech Mastny, ed. (Westport, Conn.: Greenwood Press, 1984) and "Trends in the Conventional Arms Trade," *National Forum*, Special issue on "The Militarization of the Globe" (Fall 1986).

3. For the purposes of this paper, "prewar period" refers to the two to three years prior to the outbreak of hostilities. The dollar values for those years are summed and averaged in the following tables.

4. Afghanistan, Somalia, Vietnam, Iraq, Syria, Iran, and Israel.

5. For the purposes of this study, a long war is one in which armed hostilities continue for two years or more. The dollar values for those years are summed and averaged in the following tables.

6. Even Nicaragua is not an exception. Although tables 3 and 4 suggest that Nicaragua changed its procurement patterns during hostilities, in fact, the Nicaraguan government altered its bloc orientation only after the Sandinista victory in 1979 and before the current confrontation with its neighbors. Despite the initial willingness of the United States to continue providing military assistance, the Sandinista government drew closer to Eastern bloc suppliers for political and ideological reasons. Unlike the other cases, the change in its procurement pattern was not due to war-connected supplier restrictions or demands and occurred before the cross-border conflict reached its current levels of intensity.

7. This figure probably underestimates Soviet deliveries to Nicaragua. Bulgaria has shipped almost as much equipment to Nicaragua as the Soviet Union, and according to a State Department analyst interviewed in March 1986, "Bulgaria was only a shipper," so Nicaragua's dependence upon the USSR undoubtedly is considerably higher than 56 percent.

8. Exceptions are Argentina and Iran, which were embargoed by their former principal suppliers, and Honduras. The war period for Argentina, however, lasted only one and a half months, and its military purchases in the months following more than compensated for any interruption in deliveries. The apparent "decline" in wartime military assistance to Honduras is due to an unusually large procurement during the prewar period. Israel completed delivery of "an air force" (Mystère fighters and Arava transports) in 1978, which constituted more than half of total Honduran military expenditures for that period.

9. Central Intelligence Agency (CIA), *Arms Flows to LDCs: U.S.-Soviet Comparisons, 1974-77*, ER 78-10494U (Washington, D.C.: CIA, November 1978), 5. Twelve to 18 months have generally elapsed between sales agreements and deliveries of Soviet weapons; U.S. lead times have averaged about three years.

10. Soviet military production of major weapon systems, particularly tanks, missiles, and fighter aircraft, is much larger than that of the United States. For production figures, see "Soviet military production outstrips the West's," *Flight International* (September 26, 1981), 927–929. According to one source, the Soviet Union now has the largest military industrial base in the world, which is composed of 150 major plants throughout the USSR, which are supported by thousands of feeder plants. U.S. Department of Defense, *Soviet Military Power, 1983* (Washington, D.C.: GPO), 72.

11. Andrew J. Pierre, "Arms Sales: The New Diplomacy," in *International Issues and Perspectives* (Washington, D.C.: National Defense University, 1983), 215.

12. The foregoing discussion is based on remarks delivered at Columbia University by Morton S. Miller, a U.S. State Department official in October 1985 and supplemented by information culled from *Jane's All the World's Aircraft, 1984-85*, John W. Taylor, ed. (London: Jane's Publishing Inc., 1984). For a description of the Soviet sea and airlift effort, see "Soviet Arms for Ethiopia Jam Sealanes," *Washington Post*, January 20, 1978.

13. The size of the Soviet resupply of Syria after the Lebanon

war, which began in December 1982, is not reflected in table 5 because the dollar values for 1983 are only conservative "best" estimates based on mid-1983 figures.

14. See appendix 2. Comparing force structures and acquisitions without taking into account attrition or depreciation rates can give a distorted picture of the actual number of arms transfers taking place. For some countries, although there is no noticeable increase in number of weapon systems, replacements for old systems have been purchased and integrated into inventories. Thus dollar values for arms can rise while the number of weapons in inventory remains stable.

In general, attrition and depreciation are relatively high in the Third World, according to Leiss, et al., ranging from 10 percent for combat aircraft, trainers, and helicopters to 5 percent for armored cars, armored personnel carriers, and ships. (In comparison, the attrition ratio for combat aircraft in the United States is about 5 percent.) During wartime, however, the rate is even higher. Somalia's air force, for example, declined by 17 percent during the first year of the Ethiopian-Somalian war and 60 percent during the second year.

15. Steven David, "Realignment in the Horn: The Soviet Advantage," *International Security* 4, no. 2 (Fall 1979): 69–90.

16. International Institute for Strategic Studies (IISS), *The Military Balance, 1979–80* through *1983–84* (London: IISS).

17. Robert G. Neumann, "Assad and the Future of the Middle East," *Foreign Affairs* 62, no. 3 (Winter 1983–84): 237–256.

18. Anthony H. Cordesman, "Soviet-Syrian Challenge," *Near East Report* (October 14, 1983), 24, 33. According to the *Wall Street Journal*, the SA-5 batteries were delivered in October 1982 at a cost of $2 billion, the SS-21s at a cost of $3 billion, and $1 billion was paid to improve Syria's command and control capabilities, all financed by Saudi Arabia. ("One Hard Lesson," *Wall Street Journal*, November 9, 1983). See also Drew Middleton, *New York Times*, January 7, 1984, p. 4; IISS, *The Military Balance, 1983–84*; Eugene Kozicharow, "Navy Blames Aircraft Loss on Soviet Sensor Change," *Aviation Week and Space Technology* (December 12, 1983), 23.

There is some difference of opinion over when the Soviets delivered what to the Syrians. One military analyst claims the SA-9 had been in Syria's inventory prior to the Lebanon war and that numerous SA-8/9 launchers were knocked out during the summer of 1982. See W. Seth Carus, "The Military Lessons of the 1982 Israel-Syria Conflict," *The Lessons of Recent Wars in the Third World: Approaches and Case Studies*, vol. 1, Robert E. Harkavy and Stephanie G. Neuman, eds. (Lexington, Mass.: Lexington Books, 1985), 263. The SS-21, according to the IISS, *Military Balance, 1984-85*, arrived sometime after July 1984.

19. The capabilities of Soviet and U.S. equipment made during the same year are not necessarily comparable. The age factor is introduced here only as a rough indicator of the technological sophistication of the combatants' inventories relative to each other and their suppliers.

20. On U.S. training objectives, see Ernest W. Lefever, "The Military Assistance Training Program," *Annals*, 424 (March 1976), 85-95; U.S. Congress, Committee on Foreign Affairs, "Military Assistance Training," report of the Subcommittee on National Security Policy and Scientific Developments, April 2, 1971. For a similar assessment of Soviet goals, see Daniel S. Papp, "Soviet Military Assistance to Eastern Europe," in *Communist Nations' Military Assistance*, John F. Copper and Daniel S. Papp, eds. (Boulder, Colo.: Westview Press, 1983), 31.

21. The breakdown of these categories of U.S. military assistance is as follows: support equipment – 18 percent; spare parts and modifications – 18 percent; and support services – 26 percent. "Support equipment" is composed of nonlethal, or dual-use items such as trucks, communications equipment, and cargo aircraft. (Defense Security Assistance Agency [DSAA], *Weapons Analysis Report*; Interview with DSAA official, June 1985.) The Soviet statistical breakdown was provided by Dr. Andrew Semmel, Department of Defense, March 1984.

22. Roger E. Kanet, "Soviet Military Assistance to the Third World," *Communist Nations' Military Assistance*, 39-71.

23. George E. Hudson, "The Economics of Soviet Arms Transfers: A Policy Dilemma," paper prepared for presentation at a meeting of the Seminar on Soviet and East European International Economic Behavior, Mershon Center, Ohio State University, May 3, 1984, pp. 19-20.

24. Data are not available for the dollar value of Soviet-Warsaw Pact training programs. It can be assumed, however, given the disparity in numbers of personnel trained, that the dollar value is considerably less than that of the United States.

25. Interview with State Department official, October 1985.

26. "Soviet maintenance in Afghanistan," *Jane's Defence Weekly* (March 1, 1986), 367–368.

27. The Lebanon war is an anomaly in which Israel retained both the quantitative and qualitative edge.

28. The superpowers have responded similarly in other wars not considered in this study. For example, at the beginning of the 1973 Middle East war, both the United States and the USSR practiced restraint. Unprecedented rates of high attrition in combat equipment prompted pleas for resupply from both sides. But from the onset of the war on October 6 until October 12, the United States adopted a wait and see attitude until the political and diplomatic smoke cleared. Kissinger is quoted as saying: "We tried to talk in the first week. When that didn't work, we said, fine, we'll start pouring in equipment until we create a new reality." U.S. resupply began on October 13; the Soviet's had begun two days earlier. See Lewis Sorley, *Arms Transfers Under Nixon: A Policy Analysis* (Lexington, Ky.: The University Press of Kentucky, 1983), 89–95.

29. William Lewis, "Ethiopia-Somalia (1977–1978)" in *Lessons of Recent Wars*, 102–106.

30. Ibid., 113–114; DSAA, *Fiscal Year Series, 1983*.

31. U.S. Senate, Committee on Foreign Relations, *War in the Gulf*, a staff report, August 1984, p. 10. At the same time, the Soviets offered military and other forms of assistance to Iran. But despite Soviet efforts, Iran during the early 1980s took a consistently anti-Soviet position, rejecting direct military aid and suppressing the pro-Moscow Tudeh Party. According to the Senate report, however, the Soviet resumption of arms exports to Iraq may have been too late. Although the Soviets subsequently delivered several billion dollars worth of military equipment to Iraq, "the Iraqis will not forget that the Soviet Union embargoed weapons and sided with Iran in the early stages of the war." A great deal of distrust between Iraq and the Soviet Union remains. Dennis Ross, "Soviet Views Toward the Gulf War," *Orbis* 28, no. 3 (Fall 1984): 437–447.

32. Vladimir N. Sakharov, "Soviets pursue a wary Iran-Iraq war policy line," *San Diego Union*, July 22, 1984, p. C-7. For further discussion of Soviet moderation in the transfer of offensive weapons such as surface-to-surface and air-to-surface missiles, see "Iraq: Those Reports of New Weapons," *Defense and Foreign Affairs Daily*, June 25, 1984, pp. 1–2; John Kifner, *New York Times*, July

17, 1984; "USA and Soviets Balancing Arms Sales to Iran/Iraq," *Jane's Defence Weekly* (July 21, 1984), 60.

33. "Soviets Reportedly Replace Syria's Summer Weapons Losses," *Washington Post*, December 3, 1982; "One Hard Lesson," *Wall Street Journal*, November 9, 1983; Cordesman, "Soviet-Syrian Challenge," 33; Alexander J. Bennett, "Arms Transfers as an Instrument of Soviet Policy in the Middle East," *The Middle East Journal* 39, no. 4 (Autumn 1985): 745–774.

34. Michael Richardson, "The F-16 for Southeast Asia: Arms race or strategic balance?" *Pacific Defence Reporter* (May 1985), 17–19; "New Arms, Troops Expand Soviet Military Role in Southeast Asia," *Washington Post*, December 21, 1983, p. 1; Author interview with State Department official in January 1984. The SU-22 is a downgraded Fitter-F (1977) aircraft with a less capable engine and avionics.

35. In early 1984 the Soviet Union deployed 14 MiG-23s, 4 Bear D long-range naval reconnaissance aircraft, 4 Bear F antisubmarine warfare planes, and 16 Soviet Tu-16 Badger medium-range bombers and submarines, as well as surface and support ships at Cam Ranh Bay. Michael Richardson, "The F-16 for Southeast Asia"; Drew Middleton, *New York Times*, January 30, 1984; "New Arms, Troops Expand Soviet Military Role in Southeast Asia," *Washington Post*, December 21, 1983.

36. See table 5 for Soviet military assistance figures. Estimates of total annual Soviet expenditures on the war in Afghanistan vary widely. There is general agreement that by 1984 the Soviets had increased their financial involvement by adding new air bases and support facilities in Afghanistan. Analysts differ vigorously, however, over the percent rise and real cost of the war to the Soviets. Their estimates range from "several hundreds of millions" (author interview with State Department official, January 1986) to several billion. A British journal calculated the cost at $1.5 billion (*Economist* [July 14, 1984], 37–39, 41), whereas a Chinese report estimated that expenses had risen to $2.2 billion in 1984 (*Intelligence Digest* [March 1, 1984], 6–7). But before the buildup in 1984 and since then, even larger estimates have appeared in the literature. In 1983 and 1985, for example, different sources claimed the Soviets were spending between $3–$5 billion annually: "Afghanistan," *Bulletin of Atomic Scientists* (June–July 1983), 23; Joseph J. Collins, "The Soviet Experience in Afghanistan," *Military Review* (May 1985), 16–21; James B. Curren and Phillip A. Karber, "Afghanistan's Ordeal Puts Region At Risk,"

Armed Forces Journal International (March 1985), 78–105.

But regardless of variation, based on the Organization of Joint Chiefs of Staff's calculation of Soviet defense expenditures in 1984 – $245 billion – none of the above estimates amount to more than 1 or 2 percent of the Soviets' total military budget – a sum considerably less than that spent by the United States during the Vietnam War. As one source notes, in 1969 the U.S. war effort absorbed 23 percent of the U.S. defense budget. Curren and Karber, "Afghanistan's Ordeal Puts Region at Risk," 98.

37. By 1986, there were some indications that this might be changing. Stung by criticisms leveled at the performance of their systems during the Lebanon war, the Soviet Union may be offering favored clients more modern equipment, such as MiG-29s to India.

38. Joachim Maitre, *Wall Street Journal*, June 8, 1984, p. 29.

39. The Reagan administration had stopped exports to Israel of F-15 and F-16 fighters in 1981 after the Osiraq and Beirut bombings. The onset of the Lebanon war delayed delivery of an additional 75 F-16s from June 1982 to August 1983. "Cam Ranh Bay – forward base of the Soviet Pacific Fleet," *Jane's Defence Weekly* (July 21, 1984), 66; Drew Middleton, *New York Times*, January 30, 1984; "New Arms, Troops Expand Soviet Military Role in Southeast Asia," *Washington Post*, December 21, 1983. For a lengthier analysis of the strategic benefits accruing to the USSR, see Lief Rosenberger, "The Soviet-Vietnamese Alliance and Kampuchea," *Survey* 27 (Autumn–Winter 1983): 207–231.

40. Judith Miller, *New York Times*, February 14, 1984.

41. Ibid. Anthony Cordesman claims the 7,000 figure used by most analysts is too high and that the number of Soviet advisers in Syria is closer to 5,000. Cordesman, "Soviet-Syrian Challenge."

42. For the pros and cons of the debate, see James E. Dougherty, "The Polisario Insurgency: War and Minuet in North-West Africa," *Conflict* 2, no. 2 (1980): 93–120; John Maclean, "State Department Divided From Within Over Tank Sale to Morocco," *Defense Week* (November 3, 1980), 7; William Lewis, "War in the Western Sahara," in *Lessons of Recent Wars*, 132.

43. The shah of Iran had been deposed, President Anastasio Somaza of Nicaragua had fallen, and the Sandinistas had come to power; the Soviet Union had invaded Afghanistan; U.S. allies and conservative Arab countries were publicly questioning U.S. resolve to defend its allies and friends; some of the most vigorous congressional opponents to Moroccan aid had been electorally defeated.

44. *Defense and Foreign Affairs Daily* (April 1980), 1–2.

45. U.S. Department of Defense, "Security Assistance Programs," congressional presentation, FY 1983, p. 106; Martha Wenger, "Reagan Stakes Morocco in Sahara Struggle," *MERIP Reports* (May 1982), 22–26.

Chapter 3

1. The worldwide trade in black market arms is estimated to amount to $10 billion a year. (Michael T. Klare, "Death on the Blackmarket," *Cleveland Plain Dealer*, June 13, 1985.) Armed forces as diverse as the Afghan rebels, the Polisario insurgents, and the Israeli army have found the battlefield a rich source of supply.

2. Interviews in Lebanon, July 1982; Thomas M. Cynkin, "Aftermath of the Saur Coup: Insurgency and Counterinsurgency in Afghanistan," *The Fletcher Forum* (Summer 1982), 269–298.

3. Hedrick Smith, *New York Times*, March 28, 1984, p. A-3. See also "Guerillas Seize 20% of U.S. military aid," *Jane's Defence Weekly* (March 17, 1984), 392.

4. *SIPRI Yearbook, 1984* (London: Taylor and Francis, 1984), 199.

5. W. Seth Carus, "Defense Planning in Iraq," in *Defense Planning in Less Industrialized States*, Stephanie G. Neuman, ed. (Lexington, Mass.: Lexington Books, 1984), 38.

6. From the start of the Iran-Iraq war through 1983, France sold approximately $5 billion worth of arms to Iraq, much of it in exchange for oil. (*SIPRI Yearbook, 1984*, p. 199.) Iraq has received from France Mirage F-1 fighters (including F-1EQ5s delivered in 1984), Super Etendard planes with Exocet missiles, Exocet-armed Aerospatiale Super Frelon helicopters, antitank SA-342 Gazelle helicopters, as well as SA-330 Puma transport helicopters, large numbers of AMX-30 and AMX-10 tanks, armored vehicles, rapid firing 105-mm guns, and Crotale antiaircraft and coastal batteries. "France is Arab world's arms source," *Flight International* (October 8, 1983), 956–958; "France Reported to Send Fighters to Iraq Air Force," *New York Times*, October 9, 1983; Don Oberdorfer, *Washington Post*, January 1, 1984, p. 1; "Bahrain reports new Mirages for Iran," *Jane's Defence Weekly* (November 3, 1984), 760.

7. "Iraqi Pilots Train in Britain," *Washington Times*, May 2, 1983, p. 236.

8. Although the Iraqis are said to have wanted to purchase a long list of equipment from the United States, the State Department thus far has refused export licenses to Iraq for military equipment. There has been some speculation about the dual-use character of the 45 Bell 214ST helicopters approved for sale to Iraq in 1985. See David B. Ottaway, *Washington Post*, September 13, 1985.

9. "Iraq Claims 'Devastating' Weapon Built in Brazil," *O Estado de Sao Paulo* (in Portuguese), February 12, 1983, p. 5.

10. China has been supplying Iraq with Type 69 main battle tanks and a Chinese Type 531 full-tracked armored personnel carrier armed with a single 12.7-mm DShKM heavy machine gun. "Chinese-made APC in Iraqi service," *Jane's Defence Weekly* (March 31, 1984); "China Plays Both Sides in Persian Gulf War," *Washington Post*, January 13, 1983, p. 21.

11. Russell W. Howe, *Washington Times*, April 13, 1983; Clarence A. Robinson, Jr., "Iraq, Iran Acquiring Chinese Built Fighters," *Aviation Week and Space Technology* (April 11, 1983), 16–17.

12. *SIPRI Yearbook, 1984*, p. 199.

13. Anthony H. Cordesman, "U.S. Military Assistance to the Middle East: National Security or Election-Year Politics?" *Armed Forces Journal International* (January 1984), 26–33.

14. Gary Sick, *New York Times*, June 13, 1985.

15. "Iranians pushing to Get U.S. arms," *Philadelphia Inquirer*, August 3, 1985, p. 10.

16. Robinson, "Iraq, Iran Acquiring Chinese Built Fighters."

17. Ibid.; Drew Middleton, *New York Times*, May 28, 1984, p. 4. According to Middleton, 60 Soviet-built MiG fighters have been discussed.

18. MILAVNEWS (Aviation Advisory Services, Ltd. Stapleford Airfield, Romford, Essex, England), August 1983. It has been reported from many sources that only 35–40 of Iran's combat aircraft are operational, suggesting that Iran's efforts to purchase fighters and fighter-bombers have not been successful. See Peter Truell, *Wall Street Journal*, June 18, 1984, p. 24; Drew Middleton, *New York Times*, July 21, 1984, p. 6.

19. James R. Schiffman, *Wall Street Journal*, May 2, 1984, p. 5; Anthony H. Cordesman, "Arms Sales to Iran: A Working Note," unpublished paper, January 29, 1985, p. 5.

20. Cordesman, "Arms Sales to Iran"; Schiffman, *Wall Street*

Journal, May 2, 1984. The T-62 tank is an old Soviet model, which is no longer produced in the Soviet Union. They entered production in the Soviet Union in 1961 and ended production there in 1971–1972. *Jane's Armour and Artillery, 1984–85* (London: Jane's Publishing, Inc., 1984), 7.

21. Cordesman, "Arms Sales to Iran."

22. Ibid., 6. According to Cordesman, Libya has delivered T-54/55 or T-62 tanks, artillery shells, SA-7 missiles, and artillery (120-mm and 130-mm).

23. "Arms Merchants in the Gulf War," *MERIP Reports* (July–September 1984), 39–40; Schiffman, *Wall Street Journal*, May 2, 1984; "Iranian's Pushing to Get U.S. Arms," *Philadelphia Inquirer*, August 3, 1985, p. 10.

24. "Syrian planes carrying 'arms to Iran,'" *Jane's Defence Weekly* (May 26, 1984), 812.

25. "Arms Being Sold to Iran Through Intermediaries," *O Estado de Sao Paulo* (in Portuguese), June 12, 1984, p. 2.

26. Ibid.

27. According to Cordesman, the Chinese transfers included artillery, ammunition, rockets, and other items "whose source is not readily identifiable." Cordesman, "Arms Sales to Iran," p. 6. See also "Arms Merchants in the Gulf War," *MERIP Reports* (July–September, 1984), 39–40.

28. Although U.S. military exports to both sides have been barred since the war's inception, some U.S.-supplied parts for U.S.-made civilian aircraft and transportation and oil-field equipment have been transferred commercially. U.S. exports to Iran during the first 10 months of 1982 were $87 million and during the same period of 1983 were $161 million. Several times that amount of U.S.-made goods are believed to be delivered to Iran through indirect trade involving third countries. Don Oberdorfer, *Washington Post*, January 1, 1984.

29. *Der Spiegel*, November 21, 1983, p. 16, cited in *SIPRI Yearbook, 1984*, p. 199.

30. Exceptions are several items delivered to Iran by the West Europeans that were on order prior to the Iranian revolution.

31. Drew Middleton, *New York Times*, July 21, 1984, p. 6; Peter Truell, *Wall Street Journal*, June 18, 1984, p. 27.

32. U.S. Senate, Committee on Foreign Relations, *War in the Gulf*, 1, 3.

33. On April 2, 1982 Britain broke diplomatic relations with

Argentina and on April 9, the EEC instituted a Community-wide ban on arms deliveries to Argentina. On April 30, the United States announced it had ordered sanctions against Argentina and would respond favorably to requests for material support for British forces. *Keesings Contemporary Archives* (*Keesings*) (London: Longman Group Ltd.), 31529, 31532, 31709.

34. Slaughter, "The Politics and Nature of the Conventional Arms Transfer Process."

35. Interview with State Department official, December 1985.

36. Slaughter, "The Politics and Nature of the Conventional Arms Transfer Process."

37. Lawrence S. Germain documents the many launchings of special Soviet intelligence space craft during the Falklands conflict. See his "Appendix: A Diary of the Falklands Conflict," *Military Lessons of the Falkland Islands War: Views from the United States*, Bruce W. Watson and Peter M. Dunn, eds. (Boulder, Colo.: Westview Press, 1984), 139–161. The Argentines have denied receiving any satellite information from the Soviets, however, pointing out that they lacked the necessary communication links. F. Clifton Berry, Jr., "Foreword," *Military Lessons of the Falkland Islands War.*

38. Robert W. Duffner, "Conflict in the South Atlantic: the impact of air power," *Air University Review* (March/April 1984), 79–87.

39. Michael Getler, *Washington Post*, January 24, 1978.

40. Jonathan Broder, *Chicago Tribune*, February 12, 1978, p. 6; Brophy O'Donnell, *Baltimore Evening Sun.* February 21, 1978, p. 10. Israel's assistance has continued in the postwar period reportedly through a trading company based in Ethiopia headed by an Israeli ex-colonel. "Ethiopia 'relies on Israel for arms,'" *Jane's Defence Weekly* (January 26, 1985), 124.

41. David, "Realignment in the Horn," 86; *Politika* (Belgrade) (March 23, 1978) quoted in *Keesings*, May 26, 1978, p. 28991.

42. Philip Taubman, *New York Times*, July 21, 1983, p. 1.

43. Jean-Pierre Langellier, *Manchester Guardian*, (excerpted from *Le Monde*), May 6, 1984, p. 8. According to one account, both Saudi Arabia and Israel were asked to give covert financial support to the Contras. Saudi Arabia declined to do so, and Israel has denied involvement. U.S. sources report that by 1984, however, Israeli assistance totaled several million dollars and was reaching the Contras indirectly through a South American intermediary.

There has also been speculation that the United States might be repaying Israel for this unofficial aid in its military and economic aid package to Israel. Bob Woodward, *Washington Post*, May 19, 1984, p. 1.

44. A flood of press reports about these activities has appeared in a variety of sources – Israel's *Haaretz* and the *Jerusalem Post* as well as U.S., English, Lebanese, and Chinese publications. Reference to Israeli press items appeared in Claudia Wright, "A back door to war," *New Statesman* (August 5, 1983), 16–17 and "Israeli-Latin Role Is Denied by U.S.," *New York Times*, April 22, 1984. *Xinhua*, July 30, 1983 observed that Israel "plays a supplementary role to U.S. actions" in Central America, quoting a Lebanese magazine that Israel "will provide support when Washington, out of regional political considerations, finds it inconvenient to support a [pro-U.S.] regime." See also Langellier, *Manchester Guardian; Jane's Defence Weekly* (February 23, 1985), 291; Leslie H. Gelb, *New York Times*, December 17, 1982, p. 1; Taubman, *New York Times*, July 21, 1983, p. 1; Taubman, *New York Times*, January 13, 1985, p. 1.

45. Civilian activities have included the donation of money to Nicaraguan rebels by private U.S. citizens and corporations and the shipment of military equipment to the Contras and to El Salvador's forces by an Alabama-based veterans organization called Civilian Military Assistance. "Ex-U.S. Intelligence and Military Personnel Supply Anti-Nicaraguan Rebels," *New York Times*, November 8, 1983, p. 12; Taubman, *New York Times*, September 10, 1984, p. 10.

46. Jackson Diehl, *Washington Post*, June 10, 1984, p. 1. Peter Hellyer, "Brazil's increased arms sales include Iraq-Iran deals," *Jane's Defence Weekly* (June 23, 1984), 1012.

47. Jack Anderson, *Washington Post*, November 20, 1983.

48. "Quaddafi Embraces Morocco, but Algeria Is Coy," *Washington Times*, August 16, 1984, p. 6; Louis Eaks, "Polisario offensive in Morocco's guerilla war," *Jane's Defence Weekly* (October 27, 1984), 720. See also Jonathan Broder, *Chicago Tribune*, August 16, 1985.

49. William Lewis, "War in the Western Sahara," 130.

50. Martha Wenger, "Reagan Stakes Morocco in Sahara Struggle," *MERIP Reports* (May 1982), 25; "Placating the Saudis by Arming Morocco," *Long Island Newsday*, October 29, 1979; Al J. Ventner, "Morocco vs. Polisario in the Sahara Desert Shakedown," *Soldier of Fortune* (December 1980), 36–38.

51. U.S. military and economic aid fluctuated between approximately $53 million and $81 million during the Carter administration. It began rising into the $90 million range in 1981 and 1982, reaching a peak of $124 million in 1983 after King Hassan agreed in May 1982 to access and transit rights in emergency contingencies for U.S. forces. Department of Defense, congressional presentation, *Security Assistance Program FY 1976-FY 1986*; *Jane's Defence Weekly* (November 24, 1984), 915; ACDA, *World Military Expenditures and Arms Transfers*, 1973-77 – 1985.

52. "CIA Funnels Small Arms to Afghans," *Philadelphia Inquirer*, June 8, 1980; MILAVNEWS, July 1983; "Afghan Rebel Aid," *Aviation Week and Space Technology* (May 28, 1984), 15.

53. In 1984 a large number of reports about the size of U.S. aid to the Afghan rebels appeared. Differing widely, they established only that the dollar value of the U.S. commitment had risen. Starting at $50 million (*Wall Street Journal*, July 27, 1984), published estimates rose to "approximately $150 million a year." "Afghan Rebel Aid," *Aviation Week and Space Technology* (May 28, 1984), 15. See also, "Caravans on Moonless Nights," *Time*, June 11, 1984, pp. 38-40; "More Aid Voted for Afghan Rebels," *Washington Post*, July 28, 1984, p. 1.

54. The supply patterns to the Afghan guerrillas are described in Richard Halloran, *New York Times*, January 17, 1980, p. 3; "Egypt Says It Is Training Afghans," *New York Times*, February 14, 1980; "U.S. Supplying Afghan Insurgents," *New York Times*, February 16, 1980; "U.S. Weapons for Afghanistan," *Chicago Tribune*, July 22, 1981; "Caravans on Moonless Nights," *Time*, June 11, 1984.

55. Remarks attributed to Dr. Hashmatullah Mojadidi, the son of a rebel leader during a trip to the United States. "Soviet Troops Are Defecting," *Washington Times*, December 1, 1983, p. 5.

56. "Afghans Plan USSR Terror Attacks," *Jane's Defence Weekly* (March 31, 1984), 481-484.

57. Taubman, *New York Times*, July 21, 1983. According to the article, these are Defense Intelligence Agency estimates that were included in secret parts of a General Accounting Office report published in June 1983. Because the PLO did not have much armor, the list probably refers to the total number of weapons captured during the Lebanon war, Syrian as well as PLO. Most of the small arms, mortars, hand grenades, rockets, etc., however, represent PLO arms discovered and taken by the Israelis from hidden caches in Lebanon.

58. Author interview, December 1983.

59. Norman Kempster, *International Herald Tribune*, July 31–August 1, 1982, p. 2; "Supermarket of Death," *Newsview*, August 24, 1982; "Basic Facts: The IDF and the Security of Israel," *IDF Spokesman*, (Israeli Defense Forces) April 1982, p. 43; Author briefings by IDF officers, August 1982.

60. "Basic Facts," *IDF Spokesman*, April 1982, p. 44; Author briefings, August 1982.

61. IDF-translated document captured during Lebanon war, June 30, 1982, provided by the IDF to the author, August 1982.

62. Richard Schultz contributed the following three-part typology in his article: "The Role of External Forces in Third World Conflicts," *Comparative Strategy* 4, no. 2 (1983): 70–184.

63. Claudia Wright, "A back door to war," *New Statesman* (August 5, 1983), 16–17.

64. An interview with a captured PLO terrorist revealed that training in the Soviet Union included instructions in the use of AK-47 Kalashnikov assault rifles and other light arms, explosives, command techniques, and topography and concentrated on "theory" and "tactics." William Claiborne, *Washington Post*, November 17, 1980, p. 17.

65. *Economist* (July 10, 1982), 48.

66. Schultz, "The Role of External Forces," 98; Yonah Alexander, *Miami Herald*, December 11, 1985, p. 1-E.

67. Don Shannon, *Los Angles Times*, April 16, 1981, p. B-1.

68. "Nicaraguan Foes of Regime Train . . . ," *New York Times*, January 18, 1982, p. 1. John Russell of the U.S. Justice Department is quoted as saying "We're not condoning it, [but] the neutrality laws have a lot of loopholes [and for individuals merely to undertake] paramilitary exercises using permitted weapons doesn't constitute a violation of law."

69. Edward Cody, *Washington Post*, February 14, 1980, p. 1.

70. Leiss, et al., *Arms Transfers to Less Developed Countries*, 236, provide the figures for the 1960s. According to the U.S. comptroller general, in 1975 the proportion of U.S. military advisers in LDCs was 92 percent. Comptroller General, *Assessment of Overseas Advisory Efforts of the U.S. Security Assistance Program, Report to the Congress* (Washington, D.C.: Departments of Defense and State, October 31, 1975), 47.

71. CIA, *Handbook of Economic Statistics, 1976.* The 1975 figure does not include 1,210 Chinese military technicians in Africa and

the Middle East; U.S. State Department, *Soviet and East European Aid to the Third World, 1981* (Washington, D.C.: Bureau of Intelligence and Research, February 1983). The 1981 figure does not include 39,175 Cuban military technicians in Africa, Latin America, and the Middle East.

72. Some reports claim Cubans are also engaged in combat. "Cubans executed 360 villagers in raid . . . ," *Chicago Tribune*, May 6, 1985, p. 7.

73. East German advisers are said to have played a key role in helping Ethiopia set up an internal security system. Ian Greig, "East Germany's Continuing Offensive in the Third World," paper distributed to the Foreign Affairs Research Institute, June 1982, pp. 1–8. See also *Politika* (March 23, 1978), quoted in *Keesings*, May 26, 1978, p. 28991.

74. David, "Realignment in the Horn."

75. Rosenberger, "The Soviet-Vietnamese Alliance and Kampuchea."

76. Jonathan Broder, *Chicago Tribune*, November 27, 1983.

77. Interview with State Department officials, December 1984.

78. Al J. Ventner, "Morocco vs. Polisario in the Sahara Desert Shakedown," 36–38.

79. U.S. Departments of State and Defense, *Background Paper: Central America*, May 27, 1983, pp. 16–17. See also "Cubans Bolster Military Presence," *Washington Times*, April 12, 1984, p. 1.

80. Bishara Bahdah, *Chicago Tribune*, June 21, 1983, p. 11.

81. *Jane's Defence Weekly* (June 29, 1985), 1274.

82. Drew Middleton, *New York Times*, December 5, 1983, p. 12.

83. Although not part of our sample here, a good example of this type of activity can be found within Sub-Saharan Africa where Soviet, East German, and Cuban personnel have been involved in training and advising at base areas close to areas of conflict for some years. Schultz, "The Role of External Forces," 99.

84. Ibid., 100. Training is said to normally last 3–6 months.

85. Christopher Dickey, *Washington Post*, May 23, 1983, p. 15.

86. Philip Taubman, *New York Times*, May 27, 1983. In the past, soldiers from El Salvador were trained primarily in El Salvador and the United States and a few at U.S. bases in Panama. Gerald F. Seib and Walter S. Mossberg, *Wall Street Journal*, August 17, 1983, p. 1.

87. "Guerillas Train in Pakistan to Oust Afghan Government,"

Washington Post, February 2, 1979, p. 23; Joel Brinkley, *New York Times*, April 22, 1984.

88. Howe, *Washington Times*, April 13, 1983.

Chapter 4

1. Reported in MILAVNEWS, April 1983.

2. Harry G. Summers, Jr., "Ground Warfare Lessons," in *Military Lessons of the Falkland Islands War: Views from the United States*, eds. Bruce W. Watson and Peter M. Dunn (Boulder, Colo.: Westview Press, 1984), 70; Jeffrey Ethell and Alfred Price, *Air War South Atlantic*, (London: Sidgwick & Jackson, 1983), 223.

3. MILAVNEWS, December 1982.

4. MILAVNEWS, December 1982 and June 1983. Argentina had two counterinsurgency (COIN)/training squadrons of Pucaras in inventory; apparently one was based on the Falklands and one on the mainland. (See, International Institute for Strategic Studies [IISS], *Military Balance, 1981–1982*, [London, IISS, 1981], 92.)

5. David C. Isby, "Falklands War Weapons: The Best Men and Arms Won," *Soldier of Fortune* (August 1983): 36, 69. According to Isby the British Scorpion and Scimitar exert "only half the ground pressure of a penguin. They could traverse the boggy Falklands terrain where other vehicles immediately got stuck and troops sank to their knees." (p. 69.)

6. MILAVNEWS, March 1983 and February 1983, p. 2.

7. During the war, Argentina learned the consequences of having too few maritime surveillance patrol planes in inventory. In response to that requirement, Argentina since the war has purchased four Lockheed Electra aircraft in the United States for conversion into maritime patrol planes. They are to be fitted with "state-of-the-art surface detection radar," which Argentina purchased separately. The air force also is said to have evaluated the purchase of a new fighter-bomber from the United States or France and helicopters from France. And in 1983, Argentina was scheduled to receive the first of four frigates being built in West Germany and the first of two submarines. "Argentina restocks arsenal with Tip-top fighters, missiles," *Christian Science Monitor*, January 12, 1983, p. 4.

8. Vietnam produces a light machine gun and some grenades.

9. June Teufel Dreyer, "China's Military Power in the 1980s,"

a paper distributed by the China Council of the Asia Society, August 1982.

10.   James B. Linder and A. James Gregor, "The Chinese Communist Air Force in the 'Punitive' War Against Vietnam," *Air University Review* (September/October 1981), 67–77.

11.   Quoted in Dreyer, "China's Military Power in the 1980s," 11.

12.   China received U.S. authorization to buy military hardware in June 1984. The first U.S. sale reported in August 1985 was for gas turbine engines to be used in two Chinese-designed and built destroyers. A second agreement followed in September 1985, which involved about $100 million in sales of equipment and technical help to modernize a large caliber artillery plant. Included in the sale were about $6 million worth of fuses, primers, and detonators for 155-mm artillery. China has also purchased 24 Sikorsky dual-use transport helicopters for $140 million. Kerry B. Dumbaugh and Richard F. Grimmett, *U.S. Arms Sales to China* (Washington, D.C.: Library of Congress, Congressional Research Service, July 8, 1985), 16; Paul Mann, "Study Forecasts No Change in Weapons Sales to China," *Aviation Week and Space Technology* (July 15, 1985), 24–25; "China to Receive Military Goods Under FMS," *Aviation Week and Space Technology* (September 30, 1985), 82; "U.S. Reported Close to Arms Sale to China to Modernize Air Force," *New York Times*, January 25, 1986.

13.   "Secret military deals between Israel and China," *Jane's Defence Weekly* (November 24, 1984), 915. Chinese tanks have been reported to have new Israeli-made cannons mounted on them.

14.   Quoted in Dreyer, "China's Military Power in the 1980s," 22.

15.   Some of the issues presented here are discussed at greater length in Robert E. Harkavy and Stephanie G. Neuman, "Israel," in *Arms Production in Developing Countries*, James Everett Katz, ed. (Lexington, Mass.: Lexington Books, 1984), 193–224.

16.   See, among others, *Military Electronics/Countermeasures*, special edition (January 1983), 106–145; "Lessons of Lebanon," *Defence Attaché*, no. 4/1982, pp. 23–35.

17.   See, for instance, Edward Luttwak, "Gauging Soviet Arms," *New York Times*, December 31, 1982; "Lessons of Lebanon," *Defence Attaché*.

18.   Author interview with U.S. Department of Defense official, April 1983; Anthony H. Cordesman, "The Sixth Arab-Israeli Conflict; Military Lessons for American Defense Planning," *Armed Forces Journal International* (August 1982), 29–32. The extent to

which Israel's defense industries are dependent upon the U.S. largesse is suggested by the financial assistance Israel has sought for its two major programs. U.S. FMS funds were used to help finance the domestic development and production of the Merkava tank (author interview with General Tal in Tel Aviv, August 1982) and more recently the Lavi aircraft. "Major boost for Israel's Lavi plans," *Jane's Defence Weekly* (March 3, 1984), 311; "U.S. Offers Israel More Military Aid," *Washington Times*, December 12, 1983.

19. Author interviews with Israeli defense industry officials in Tel Aviv, August 1982; Richard A. Gabriel, "Lessons of War: The IDF in Lebanon," *Military Review* 64, no. 8 (August 1984): 47–65.

20. "Pentagon Eyes Robot Planes After Israeli Success," *Chicago Tribune*, December 5, 1982, p. 14-B. The article refers to the U.S. Aquila program. The Israeli product is smaller and called a mini-RPV. For a discussion of Israel's production experience with RPVs, see Kenneth Munson, "RPVs – Who are the real remote pilots?" *Jane's Defence Weekly* (August 24, 1985), 360–361.

21. John R. McQuestion, "Attack Helicopter Operations," *Asian Defence Journal* (March 1982), 62–69.

22. Carus, "The Military Lessons of the 1982 Israel-Syria Conflict," *Lessons of Recent Wars*, 270.

23. Author correspondence with W. Seth Carus, September 22, 1985. For a detailed description of the conjunction of weapons and tactics see ibid., 264–265.

24. W. Seth Carus, "The Bekaa Valley Campaign," *Washington Quarterly* 4, no. 4 (Autumn 1982): 38.

25. *Military Electronics/Countermeasures*.

26. Carus, "The Bekaa Valley Campaign," and "The Military Lessons of the 1982 Israel-Syria Conflict," 264.

27. There has been some disagreement over the role played by various aircraft during the Lebanon war. General W. L. Creech, in his review of Israeli operations during the Lebanon war, praised the high reliability and serviceability achieved by the IDF's U.S. F-15s and the F-16s employed "every morning." But in Israel it was claimed that these planes "played a relatively small part in the overall activity." The main workhorses were said to be the IAI Kfir, making its first large-scale operational debut; the Phantom, using new inertial platforms and weapons-aiming systems for pre-

cision attacks against missile sites, artillery, tanks, and other battlefield targets; and Skyhawks equipped with similar systems for close support. MILAVNEWS, November 1982, p. 5.

28. "Israelis Report Using New Type of Missile in Lebanon War," *New York Times*, February 27, 1983, p. A-15.

29. "Elbit's artillery C3 system," *Defence Attaché*, no. 4/1982, p. 41.

30. "155mm MR Fuze from Telkoor," *Defence Attaché*, no. 4/1982, p. 45; Carus, "The Bekaa Valley Campaign," 39.

31. Clyde Owan, "The Arab-Israeli Naval Imbalance," *U.S. Naval Institute Proceedings* (March 1983), 101–109.

32. "Israeli Combat Experience Incorporated in Latest Anti-Ship Missile," *Flight International* (December 26, 1981), 1886.

33. From the Israeli viewpoint, a short war with minimal casualties is an important military goal. Innovations and technologies, especially in electronic warfare, that provide the Israelis with the ability to react quickly and save lives have a high payoff and are considered a decided military advantage. For them the process and outcome of war are inseparable.

34. Cordesman, "The Sixth Arab-Israeli Conflict," 31; Author interviews with Departments of State and Defense officials, December 1983 and January 1984.

35. Author interview with State Department official, March 24, 1983. The point made here by the informant is that, because of the superior Israeli training, education, and organization, even if the weapons were exchanged, the Israeli military would be able to extract 100 percent efficiency from the Syrians' Soviet equipment, whereas the Syrian army, already experiencing operational difficulties with what they had, would have been further handicapped by the more sophisticated U.S.-Israeli technologies.

36. Israel produces much of its army's needs in small arms and ammunitions. The Galil assault rifle and UZI submachine gun are both of indigenous design and manufacture and are standard issue for the IDF. The Israeli army, however, also uses the U.S. M-16 rifle in large numbers. See *Jane's Infantry Weapons, 1983–84* (London: Jane's Publishing Inc., 1983), 167, for a detailed description of Israeli small arms.

37. Richard Halloran, *New York Times*, July 9, 1984.

38. Dreyer, "China's Military Power in the 1980s"; Lindner and Gregor, "The Chinese Communist Air Force."

Chapter 5

1. Rodney W. Jones and Steven A. Hildreth, *Modern Weapons and Third World Powers* (Boulder, Colo.: Westview Press, 1984), 62.

2. Martin van Creveld, in his excellent book on the subject, defines logistics as "the practical art of moving armies and keeping them supplied." *Supplying War: Logistics from Wallenstein to Patton* (Cambridge: Cambridge University Press, 1977), 1–2. See also Richard A. Gabriel, "Lessons of War: The IDF in Lebanon."

3. Gabriel, "Lessons of War: The IDF in Lebanon," 45.

4. Ibid.

5. Drew Middleton, *New York Times*, December 5, 1983, p. 12.

6. Carus, "The Military Lessons of the 1982 Israel-Syrian Conflict," 266.

7. Drew Middleton, *New York Times*, December 5, 1983.

8. Interview with State Department official, December 1983.

9. Quoted in Drew Middleton, *New York Times*, January 7, 1984, p. 4.

10. Cordesman, "U.S. Military Assistance to the Middle East: National Security or Election-Year Politics?"

11. Edgar O'Ballance, "The Battle for the Hawizah Marshes: March 1985," *Asian Defence* (June 1985), 4.

12. Robert Selle, "Iran said to be training pilots for suicide strikes against U.S.," Free Press International News Service, January 9, 1984.

13. *MILAVNEWS*, August 1983.

14. Conversation with U.S. industry manager who worked in Iran prior to the revolution, January 1984. The Homofars, trained in the United States and by on-site U.S. instructors, sided with the revolution, and are presumably still functioning within the Iranian military. For further discussion on the role of the human factor in the Iran-Iraq war, see William O. Staudenmaier, "Iran-Iraq" in *Lessons of Recent Wars*, 211–231.

15. Drew Middleton, *New York Times*, February 24, 1984.

16. Steven David, "Use of Surrogate Forces by Major Powers in 'Third World Wars,'" *The Lessons of Recent Wars: Comparative Dimensions*, vol. 2, Stephanie G. Neuman and Robert E. Harkavy, eds. (Lexington, Mass.: Lexington Books, 1986). The participation

of the Cuban forces in the fighting was admitted in *Granma* (the official organ of the Cuban Communist Party). The article stated that Cuban pilots, tank drivers, artillery units, and armored infantry battalions had participated. Reported in *Keesings*, March 14, 1978. See also David, "Use of Surrogate Forces," 8; William Lewis, "Ethiopia-Somalia," in *Lessons of Recent Wars*, 99–116; Zbigniew Brzezinski, *Power and Principle* (New York: Farrar, Straus, Giroux, 1983), 178–190.

17. Interviews with State Department and Defense Department officials, December 1983 and January 1984.

18. David Laitin, "The War in the Ogaden: Implications for Siyaad's Role in Somali History," *The Journal of Modern African Studies* 17, no. 1 (1979): 95–115.

19. For a description of these logistical problems, see "Somali Democratic Republic" in Colin Legum, ed., *Africa Contemporary Record: Annual Survey and Documents 1977–1978*, vol. 10 (New York: Africana Publishing Co.), B373–B400.

20. *Keesings*, February 3, 1978; William Lewis, "Ethiopia-Somalia," in *Lessons of Recent Wars*, 111.

21. There is general agreement that El Salvador's army numbered 25 thousand in 1983. There is disagreement in various sources, however, as to whether it was enlarged by 5,000 or 10,000 during 1984. Press reports also contain discrepancies over the size of the guerrilla forces. Krauss and Sereseres give a figure of 10,000, and Mallin estimates their number at approximately 6,000. See "Is El Salvador a Lost Cause for the U.S.?" *U.S. News and World Report* (December 5, 1983), 41, 44; Jay Mallin, Sr., *Washington Times*, August 30, 1984, p. 1; Clifford Krauss, *Wall Street Journal*, August 16, 1984, p. 1; Cesar Sereseres, "Lessons from Central America's Revolutionary Wars, 1972–1984," in *Lessons of Recent Wars*, 161–187.

22. Krauss, *Wall Street Journal*, August 16, 1984.

23. "Senate Study Questions a Buildup by Pentagon in Honduras," *New York Times*, February 2, 1984.

24. *U.S. News and World Report* (December 5, 1983), 44; "Salvadoran Army's struggle is worrying observers," *Philadelphia Inquirer*, December 14, 1983, p. 18-A.

25. "Salvadoran Army's struggle is worrying observers," *Philadelphia Inquirer*, December 14, 1983, p. 18-A; *U.S. News and World Report* (December 5, 1983), 44; Krauss, *Wall Street Journal*, August 16, 1984.

26. Sereseres, "Lessons from Central America's Revolutionary Wars," in *Lessons of Recent Wars*, 180.

27. James LeMoyne, *New York Times*, March 6, 1986.

28. Ibid.

29. Ibid.

30. Zalmay Khalilzad, "The Struggle for Afghanistan, " *Survey* 25, no. 2 (Spring 1980): 189-216; John K. Cooley, *Christian Science Monitor*, January 4, 1980.

31. IISS, *The Military Balance, 1977-78; 1978-79; 1980-81; 1984-85.*

32. Interview with State Department official, January 1984.

33. Unlike Soviet troops, trained during off-duty hours to maintain their equipment, especially in harsh winter weather and rugged terrain, the Afghans apparently were not in the habit of doing so. "Soviets Reportedly Take Afghan Allies' Heavy Arms," *Washington Post*, September 13, 1980, p. 19; "Afghan and Soviet Armies offer study in contrast," *Baltimore Sun*, January 17, 1980.

34. Drew Middleton, *New York Times*, January 6, 1980.

35. John Gunston, "Afghans plan USSR terror attacks," *Jane's Defence Weekly* (March 31, 1984), 481-482.

36. Khalilzad, "The Struggle for Afghanistan," 205.

37. "Rebels Said to Destroy MiGs in Afghanistan," *Washington Post*, June 19, 1985, p. 23.

38. The defection of two Afghan Mi-24 pilots who flew to Pakistan with their helicopters in July 1985 suggests a continuing morale problem.

39. Cynkin, "Aftermath of the Saur Coup: Insurgency and Counterinsurgency in Afghanistan," *The Fletcher Forum*, Summer 1982: 269-298.

40. Carl Bernstein, "U.S. Weapons for Afghanistan," *Chicago Tribune*, July 22, 1981, p. 9.

41. Drew Middleton, *New York Times*, January 23, 1983.

42. David C. Isby, "Afghanistan 1982: the war continues," *International Defense Review* (November 1982).

43. Gunston, "Afghans plan USSR terror attacks," 482.

44. The SA-7, a manned portable missile, is similar to the U.S. Redeye, although it is somewhat less sophisticated. It was first seen in action in Egypt during the six-day war in 1967. The ZU-23 is based upon an antiaircraft gun that appeared just after World War II. *Jane's Infantry Weapons, 1983-84*, p. 344, 644; *Jane's Weapon Systems, 1984-85*, p. 120.

45. *U.S. News and World Report* (June 11, 1984), 21. For

earlier references to the SA-7s see Jere Van Dyk, *New York Times*, January 12, 1982, p. 2; "Afghan SA-7s Force Change in Soviet Helicopter Tactics," *Aerospace Daily*, August 26, 1982, p. 317.

46. During an internal U.S. policy debate over aid to the Afghan rebels, those who advocated keeping the transferred weapons simple argued that heavy, more sophisticated weapons burden guerrillas, depriving them of mobility and forcing upon them unfamiliar tactics. Because sophisticated weapons are costly and difficult to replace, guerrillas will attempt to protect them. Thus, the equipment that gives them more firepower, also slows them down, depriving them of their most important tactical advantage. As of early 1986, U.S. government policy seems to reflect this position. Interviews with State Department official, December 1983 and January 1984.

47. Department of Defense, *Soviet Military Power*, 2nd. ed. (1983), 48.

48. Quoted in "Pentagon Assesses Afghan Conflict," *New York Times*, March 10, 1983, p. 2.

49. See *Soviet Military Power, 1983*, 48–51. Citing corruption among young Soviet conscripts, who sell arms, equipment, and gasoline for alcohol, drugs, and other goods, this study also points to the poor morale on the battlefield where "the soldiers hesitate to leave the relative safety of armored personnel carriers to close with a highly skilled and motivated foe." See also "Soviets' 'Dirty War' in Afghanistan," *U.S. News and World Report*, December 19, 1983, 13.

50. James E. Dougherty, "The Polisario Insurgency," *Conflict* 2, no. 2 (1980): 93–120; "Morocco's Own Vietnam," *Financial Times*, May 10, 1979. These electronic devices, if seeded in the desert, can detect enemy movements.

51. Jonathan Broder, *Chicago Tribune*, August 16, 1985; Henry Kamm, *New York Times*, February 1, 1984.

52. Cited in Kamm, *New York Times*, February 1, 1984. Moroccan officials were quoted to the same effect by Judith Miller, *New York Times*, August 15, 1985, p. 1.

53. Gus Constantine, *Washington Times*, August 15, 1984, p. 1; Andrew Borowiec, *Washington Times*, August 16, 1984, p. 6; Judith Miller, *New York Times*, August 15, 1985, p. 1.

54. In addition to Libya's defection, Algeria appears to be increasingly disenchanted with the Polisario. Interview with State Department official, December 1984.

55. See *Keesings*, 1980, pp. 29870–29874.

56. Based on discussions with State Department and Pentagon officials, December 1983. See also Jonathan Broder, *Chicago Tribune*, May 31, 1983, p. 5; Harlan W. Jencks, "Lessons of a 'Lesson': China-Vietnam, 1979," in *Lessons of Recent Wars*, 149–151.

57. Jencks, 151.

58. Pao-min Chang, "The Sino-Vietnamese Conflict Over Kampuchea," *Survey* 27 (Autumn–Winter 1984): 175–206.

59. *Foreign Report*, July 14, 1983, p. 4 and July 12, 1984, pp. 5–6. According to these reports, the Chinese requested Israeli advice and assistance for its military industries in 1982 after the invasion of Lebanon. Israel is also thought to be clandestinely selling China military equipment through Hong Kong. Mainly air force and air defense items, the equipment includes air-to-air missiles, surface-to-air missiles, sensors, locating radar, head-up cockpit displays, and "possibly a point defense alert radar system." Russell W. Howe, *Washington Times*, January 24, 1985. See also "Secret military deals between Israel and China," *Jane's Defence Weekly* (November 24, 1984), 915; "Britain loses 'gun battle' against Israel," *Sunday Times* (London), October 14, 1984, p. 23.

60. Military analyst quoted in Broder, *Chicago Tribune*, May 31, 1983.

61. Cited in Jack Anderson, *Washington Post*, August 20, 1983, p. E-21.

62. David C. Isby, "Falklands War Weapons: The Best Men and Arms Won," *Soldier of Fortune* (August 1983), 32–37, 66–73; Julian S. Lake, "The South Atlantic War: A Review of the Lessons Learned," *Defense Electronics* (November 1983), 86ff.

63. The literature on the lessons learned from the Falklands war has burgeoned. Three interesting accounts are those of Harlan K. Ullman, "Profound or Perfunctory: Observations on the South Atlantic Conflict," in *Lessons of Recent Wars*, 239–260; Bruce W. Watson and Peter M. Dunn, eds., *Military Lessons of the Falkland Islands War*; Jeffrey Ethell and Alfred Price, *Air War: South Atlantic* (London: Sidgwick & Jackson, 1983).

64. IISS, *Strategic Survey 1982–1983* (London: IISS, 1983), 122.

65. Quoted in "Argentine forces lacked co-operation in Falklands, claims air force chief, *Jane's Defence Weekly* (November 30, 1985), 1174.

66. Jeffrey Record, "The Falklands War," *Washington Quarterly* 4, no. 4 (Autumn 1982): 43–51.

67. For one of the few analytical discussions on the connection between logistics and dependency, see Geoffrey Kemp, "Arms Transfers and the 'Back-End' Problem in Developing Countries," *Arms Transfers in the Modern World*, Stephanie G. Neuman and Robert F. Harkavy, eds. (New York: Praeger Publishers, 1979), 264–275.

68. See Anthony Pascal, *Are Third World Armies Third Rate? Human Capital and Organizational Impediments to Military Effectiveness* (Santa Monica, Calif.: RAND, January 1980), report P-6433, for a discussion of the socioeconomic constraints on miltary effectiveness.

69. George H. Quester, "Trouble in the Islands, Defending the Micro-States," *International Security* (Fall 1983), 142–175.

70. *MILAVNEWS*, December 1983.

71. Harlan W. Jencks, "Lessons of a 'Lesson,' China-Vietnam, 1979," 139–160; *New York Times*, February 12, 1985; *Jane's Defence Weekly* (April 14, 1985), 553.

72. Andrew Borowiec estimates the war in the Western Sahara is costing $1 million per day, not counting various crash development schemes. Mark Tessler, on the other hand, believes the amount is higher – $1.5 million per day, which consumes 40–50 percent of the annual state budget. Andrew Borowiec, *Washington Times*, August 22, 1984, p. 7; Mark Tessler, "Special Report, King Hassan of Morocco and the Union with Libya: Origins, Objectives, and Implications," *Middle East Review*, no. 2 – 1984/85 (December 1984), 1–4.

73. *MILAVNEWS*, February 1984. By March 1984, Iranian losses in the war with Iraq reportedly had reached $163,700 million, with the oil industry taking the worst loss ($53,700 million). Agricultural losses were put at $40,700 million. *Jane's Defence Weekly* (July 7, 1984), 1091.

74. Because the noncombatant debt figures were extracted from George Thomas Kurian, *The New Book of World Rankings* (New York: Facts on File, 1984) and are 1979 figures, they probably underestimate noncombatant debt ratios for 1982. In general, debt figures, whether for combatants or noncombatants, are thought to be only moderately reliable, particularly those derived from official government sources, which for a variety of reasons are interested in underestimating their value.

75. Jonathan Broder, *Chicago Tribune*, November 27, 1983.

76. Ibid. The full extent of Soviet assistance to Vietnam is

described in Lief Rosenberger, "Soviet-Vietnamese Alliance and Kampuchea," *Survey* 27 (Autumn–Winter 1983): 207–231.

77. Rosenberger, "Soviet-Vietnamese Alliance," 215; Broder, *Chicago Tribune*, November 27, 1983.

78. Rosenberger, "Soviet-Vietnamese Alliance," 214–221.

79. Broder, *Chicago Tribune*, May 31, 1983. In 1950–1960 China's defense industries were producing then-current Soviet weaponry. After the Sino-Soviet split in 1960, China was cut off from the USSR and did not turn elsewhere for new military technology.

80. Harlan W. Jencks, "Lessons of a 'Lesson': China-Vietnam, 1979," 149.

81. Central Reserve Bank President Alberto Benitez said $160 million of the funds El Salvador borrowed in 1983 were used to refinance the $1.3 billion 1982 debt. The remainder went to finance local development projects, arms purchases, military training costs, and imports. "El Salvador's Foreign Debt Widened to $1.55 billion," *Wall Street Journal*, January 10, 1983, p. 22.

82. "Is El Salvador a Lost Cause for U.S.?" *U.S. News and World Report* (December 5, 1983), 44.

83. "Mexico Trends Warily Through C. American battlefields," *Financial Times*, August 23, 1984, p. 4; Stephen Kinzer, *New York Times*, March 28, 1984; Jam Mallin, Sr., *Washington Times*, April 17, 1984, p. 11.

84. *Encyclopedia Americana Annual* (Danbury, Conn.: Grolier Educational Corporation, 1981), 514.

85. Drew Middleton, *New York Times*, January 7, 1984, p. 4; "One Hard Lesson," *Wall Street Journal*, November 9, 1983.

86. "Syria Turns to Iran as Political, Financial Ally," *Washington Post*, December 29, 1984.

87. Ibid.

88. "Warsaw Pact Arms Agreements Nearly Doubled in Value in 1983," *Aviation Week and Space Technology* (April 29, 1985), 213.

89. "Prices rose by 14.9% last month," *Jerusalem Post* (International Edition), February 19–25, 1984; MILAVNEWS, February 1984.

90. *New York Times*, January 27, 1984.

91. "Israeli Officials in U.S. for Talks on Troubled Ties," *New York Times*, November 28, 1983.

92. Stanley Fischer and Herbert Stein, *Wall Street Journal*, February 26, 1986, p. 24.

93. Jeff Gerth, *New York Times*, August 2, 1985.

94. According to some reports, Iran is achieving a considerable production capability for ammunition and some spares. *MILAV-NEWS*, February 1984. For a discussion of the smuggling case, see Jeff Gerth, *New York Times*, August 2, 1985.

95. Walter Goldstein, "The War Between Iraq and Iran: A War That Can't Be Won or Ended," *Middle East Review* 17, no. 1 (Fall 1984): 41–49, 57.

96. Eliyahu Kanovsky, "The Impact of the Iran-Iraq War on World Oil Markets," *USA Today*, January 1984, pp. 14–84.

97. *Economist* (February 25, 1984), 62. In 1983, lower oil prices sent the value of Iraq's oil exports down to less than $9 billion.

98. Kanovsky, *USA Today*, January 1984; "France is Arab world's arms source," *Flight International* (October 8, 1983), 956–958. Many of these payments have gone to France. Originally Iraq paid for its purchases by supplying 25 percent of France's oil. By 1983 this was down to 3.5 percent and Iraq was reported to owe France $7 billion from arms purchases. Kuwait, Qatar, and Saudi Arabia have made up some of the difference by allowing France to lift more oil from their wells on behalf of Iraq.

99. Jonathan C. Randal, *Washington Post*, May 30, 1984.

100. U.S. Senate, Committee on Foreign Relations, *War in the Gulf*, 9–10. The $485 million Iraqi pipeline to Aqaba, Jordan will bring Iraqi oil exports up to 2.5 million barrels a day. Another pipeline is planned to Yanbu, Saudi Arabia, and a parallel pipeline is to be added to the currently functioning Turkish one.

101. "Sahara War Strains Morocco," *Washington Post*, May 30, 1977, p. 2.

102. Martha Wenger, "Reagan Stakes Morocco in Sahara Struggle," 22–23.

103. Lewis, "War in the Western Sahara," in *Lessons of Recent Wars*, 134.

104. Department of Defense, Congressional Presentation, *Security Assistance Programs, FY 1982*, 135–137.

105. *MILAVNEWS*, August 1983.

106. *Defense and Foreign Affairs Daily*, December 15, 1982, pp. 1–2. See also Ellen Laipson, "Heating up the Sahara War," *Washington Quarterly* 5, no. 1 (Winter 1982): 199–202.

107. About $400 million of PLO assets in Lebanon have been confiscated or destroyed since 1982. Judith Miller, "The PLO in

Exile," *New York Times Magazine*, August 18, 1985, p. 30; Hesh Kestin, "Terror's bottom line," *Forbes*, June 2, 1986, p. 39. There is some controversy over the size of the PLO's financial holdings. Miller claims they are estimated at more than $5 billion and that the investment portfolio earns up to $1 billion a year for the PLO. Kestin claims the PLO has holdings of no more than $1 billion producing income of no more than $100 million a year. Both agree, however, that the organization's expenses are high and that outside support is less forthcoming.

108. "Afghans for the CIA?" *Middle East* (September 1984), 8.

109. James LeMoyne, *New York Times*, January 30, 1986.

110. James LeMoyne, *New York Times*, March 6, 1986.

111. During the Falklands war, after the sinking of the Argentine cruiser *General Belgrano* by the British, Argentina's navy withdrew to the protection of its coastal waters and to all intents and purposes retired from the war. In addition, as described above, only small numbers of aircraft were committed to attacks on the British convoy. (IISS, *Strategic Survey 1982–1983*, p. 122.) Iraq and Iran have been equally careful about consigning their advanced aircraft to battle, and in Southeast Asia neither the PRC nor Vietnam used their air force during the 1979 border engagement.

112. Interview with State Department official, December 1984.

Chapter 6

1. Robert M. Cutler, Laure Despres, Aaron Karp, "Aspects of Arms Transfers and of Military Technology Transfers in East-South Relations," unpublished paper presented to the XIIth World Congress of the International Political Science Association, Paris, 15–20 July 1985, p. 6. According to the authors, the new Soviet T-80 costs three times more than the T-54 that was produced in 1949. In 1982 dollars, the average cost of an F-16A was $15.7 million and an F-15A $30.6 million, in contrast to an F-4, which between 1962–1969 sold (on average) for $2.1 million ($5.8 million in 1981). See *Military Cost Handbook, 1982* (Fountain Valley, Calif.: Data Search Associates, February 1982.)

2. John Morrocco, "U.S. Analysts Rebut Israeli Attacks on Lavi Cost Assessment Report," *Defense News* (March 10, 1986), 6.

3. For a description of this growing industry, see "The Bonanza in Upgrading Rusty Russian-Made Arms," *Business Week*, March 31, 1985, pp. 117–118.

4. Most of the major weapons that Israel sells to Latin America, for example, are old, refurbished systems (e.g., Mirage IIIs to Argentina and Mystères to Honduras).

5. Adrian J. English, *Armed Forces of Latin America: their histories, development, present strength and military potential* (London: Jane's Publishing Co., 1984), 397.

6. See Stephanie G. Neuman, "The Role of Third World Military Industries: Lessons of Recent Wars," in *Lessons of Recent Wars*, vol. 2; Geoffrey Manners, "El Salvador Arms Trade," *Jane's Defence Weekly* (October 6, 1984), 563.

7. Israel, with its high educational standards and technical skills, is an outstanding exception.

8. See "Oil's Decline Seen Curbing Soviet Plans," D-10; "Budget Cuts Expected from Saudis," D-11; "Optimism in Western Europe," D-8, in the *New York Times*, March 10, 1986; "Pressures mount on Libya's Qaddafi," *Christian Science Monitor*, September 26, 1985, p. 1.

9. In spite of shortcomings in the Soviet airlift capability, it is still second only to that of the United States and is unmatched by that of any other state in the world.

10. Steven David, "Use of Surrogate Forces by Major Powers in 'Third World War,'" in *Lessons of Recent Wars*, vol. 2; MILAV-NEWS, May 1984.

11. *Jane's Defence Weekly* (March 15, 1986), 454.

12. Milton Leitenberg, "The Impact of the Worldwide Confrontation of the Great Powers: Aspects of Military Intervention and the Projection of Military Power," *Armement-Développement-Droits De L'Homme-Désarmement* (Paris: Faculté de Droit, May 1985), 474.

13. "America's Falklands War," *Economist*, March 3, 1984, pp. 29–31.

14. George de Lama, *Chicago Tribune*, March 15, 1986.

15. "Diplomats Say Libya is Disturbed At a Lack of Support From Soviet," *New York Times*, April 14, 1986.

16. Patrick Cockburn, *Boston Globe*, September 15, 1985, p. A-11.

17. Joan Parpart Zoeter, "U.S.S.R.: Hard Currency Trade and Payment," in U.S. Congress, Joint Economic Committee, *Soviet*

Economy in the 1980s: Problems and Prospects, vol. 2, 97th Cong. 2d sess., 1982, pp. 502–504; Alexander J. Bennett, "Arms Transfers as an Instrument of Soviet Policy in the Middle East," *Middle East Journal* 39, no. 4 (Autumn 1985): 769.

18. K. K. Sharma, *Baltimore Sun*, November 10, 1983, p. 2; William Branigin, *Washington Post*, November 14, 1984, p. 21.

19. See Robert M. Cutler, et al., "Aspects of Arms Transfers and of Military Technology Transfers in East-South Relations"; Aaron Karp, "Eastern European Arms Production and Arms Transfers, 1945–1985," paper presented to the 26th International Studies Association Convention, Washington, D.C., March 5–9, 1985; Gavriel D. Ra'anan, "Surrogate Forces and Power Projection," paper prepared for the conference on "Projection of Power: Perspectives, Perceptions and Logistics," 9th annual conference of the International Security Studies Program, The Fletcher School of Law and Diplomacy, Tufts University, April 23–25, 1980; James J. Townsend, "Countering Soviet Proxy Operations," paper prepared for 25th Annual Convention of the International Studies Association, March 27–31, 1984 in Atlanta, Georgia; Leitenberg, "The Impact of the Worldwide Confrontation of the Great Powers," 406–459; Schultz, "The Role of External Forces in Third World Conflicts," *Comparative Strategy*, 1–17; Trond Gilberg, "Eastern European Military Assistance to the Third World," *Communist Nation's Military Assistance*, 72–95.

20. See Cutler, et al., "Aspects of Arms Transfers and of Military Technology Transfers," 4–5.

21. Roger E. Kanet, "Soviet and East European Arms Transfers to the Third World: Strategic, Political and Economic Factors" (Brussels: NATO, April 1983), 13, cited in ibid., 5.

22. Cutler, et al., "Aspects of Arms Transfers and of Military Technology Transfers," 16, 22.

23. Ibid., 5.

24. Gilberg, "Eastern European Military Assistance to the Third World," 83.

25. Cutler, et al., "Aspects of Arms Transfers and of Military Technology Transfers," 6.

26. Cutler, et al. claim there has been only one instance when a Warsaw Pact member transferred arms in contradiction to Soviet policy. They refer to Romania's brief support of Holden Roberto's National Front for the Liberation of Angola (FLNA) in the Angolan civil war, while the Warsaw Pact backed the Popular Movement for the Liberation of Angola (MPLA).

27. For example, the T-72 tank entered production in the USSR in 1971. Production began in Poland and Czechoslovakia in 1981 when 20 vehicles were built. Production rates have been rather slow, with 100 produced in 1982. This is in contrast to the 1,400 and 1,300 produced during the latter two years in the Soviet Union. *Jane's Armour and Artillery 1984–85*, p. 62.

28. Ibid.

29. According to ACDA, *World Military Expenditures and Arms Transfers, 1985*, Indian arms exports ranged from $10–38 million between 1973 and 1983. In 1983 there were no military exports.

30. Harry Gelman and Norman D. Levine, "The Future of Soviet-North Korean Relations" (Santa Monica, Calif.: RAND, October 1984), report T-3159.

31. MILAVNEWS, July 1985; Nick Childs, "Anniversary Offensive: Gulf Flare-up," *Jane's Defence Weekly* (March 1, 1986), 365. The terms of the transfer are still unclear, but there is some speculation that the Libyans have retained control over the maintenance and operation of the missiles. Interview with State Department officials, July 1985.

32. The Soviets clearly had other good reasons for delaying arms deliveries to Libya, such as $4–6 billion in arrearages on Libya's past agreements and Colonel Qadhafi's demand to countertrade oil in payment for weapons at a time of glut in the oil market. "Diplomats Say Libya is Disturbed At a Lack of Support From Soviet," *New York Times*, April 14, 1986.

33. "Iran Seeks to Relay Arms to Morocco," *New York Times*, May 23, 1976.

34. Bernard Weinraub, *New York Times*, March 6, 1985.

35. *Jane's Defence Weekly* (August 24, 1985), 344.

36. Edy Kaufman, "The View From Jerusalem," *Washington Quarterly* 7, no. 4 (Fall 1984): 40–51; "Argentina Sends More Weapons to Central America," *Washington Post*, June 10, 1984, p. 1; "Ortega charges Israel," *Boston Globe*, August 1985, p. 11; Philip Taubman, *New York Times*, January 13, 1985.

37. George de Lama, *Chicago Tribune*, March 15, 1986.

38. "U.K. offers military training to El Salvador," *Financial Times*, February 13, 1985, p. 4; *Jane's Defence Weekly* (February 23, 1985), 291; "W. Germany to Resume Aid to El Salvador," *Washington Post*, July 18, 1984, p. 1.

39. The $17 million sale included the 2 Alouette helicopters, 2 coastal patrol boats, 45 trucks, 100 helicopter-mounted rocket

launchers, and 7,000 rocket rounds. *Newsweek*, March 29, 1982, p. 17; Jonathan C. Randal, *Washington Post*, March 31, 1982, p. 20. For an earlier, more negative French response, see "French Say Haig Calls Managua Deal Peanuts," *New York Times*, February 12, 1982, p. 9.

40. Leslie H. Gelb, *New York Times*, July 19, 1984, pp. 1, 2.

41. *Washington Post*, January 24, 1978.

42. David Ignatius, *Wall Street Journal*, February 9, 1981, p. 1.

43. Edgar O'Ballance, "The Battle for the Hawizah Marshes: March 1985," pp. 5–10.

44. Charles J. Hanley, "In the gulf war, a high price paid for a stalemate," *Philadelphia Inquirer*, August 1, 1984, p. 2; Cordesman, "Arms Sales to Iran," 6.

45. Mansour Farhang, "The Iran-Iraq War: The Feud, the Tragedy, the Spoils," *World Policy Journal* (Fall 1985), 659–680.

46. Quoted by Roy Gutman, *Newsday*, May 20, 1984, p. 3; Hanley, *Philadelphia Inquirer*, August 1, 1984.

47. British ships (a tanker and two logistics ships), Swiss Pilatus PC-7 trainers, and the Italian-Swiss Skyguard antiaircraft system were said by their producers to fall into the category of "prerevolution" orders and were delivered. The export of Italian-produced helicopters, Ch-47s, which had been ordered by the shah, was halted by the Reagan administration when it bought the 11 helicopters still outstanding from the manufacturer. Interview with State Department official, March 1985; Cordesman, "Arms Sales to Iran," 11; "Iranian Navy Warns Against Cargoes to Iraq," *Jane's Defence Weekly* (August 10, 1985), 254.

48. "Israel halts arms supplies to Iran in New Gulf policy," *Jane's Defence Weekly* (March 30, 1985), 544; James R. Schiffman, *Wall Street Journal*, May 2, 1984, p. 5.

49. Cordesman, "Arms Sales to Iran," 6. According to some skeptics, the Chinese restraint may be only temporary. Interview with State Department official, January 1986.

50. *Army Quarterly and Defence Journal* 114 (1984): 215; *Jane's Defence Weekly* (June 30, 1984), 1058.

51. On Korea: Schiffman, *Wall Street Journal*, May 2, 1984; On Austria: Jack Anderson and Dale Van Atta, *Washington Post*, February 28, 1986, p. C-20; MILAVNEWS, February 1986; on France: Beau Morris, "Why France's Arms Exports Make It a Paper Tiger," *Armed Forces Journal* (October 1978), 19.

52. Shahram Chubin, "Israel and the Iran-Iraq War," *Inter-*

national Defense Review (March 1985), 303–304; Albert L. Weeks, *New York City Tribune*, May 1, 1985, p. 1; Interview with State Department official, November 1985.

53. Interview, August 5, 1985.

54. Townsend, "Countering Soviet Proxy Operations."

55. The prohibition against the retransfer of U.S. defense articles is contained in the U.S. Arms Export Control Act (ACEA) of 1976, as amended, cited in the Department of Defense, *Security Assistance Manual*, chapter 2, section 3 (January 2, 1985), 2.2–2.3.

56. For example, the Carter administration halted Israel's military sales to Guatemala, and during the final stages of the Nicaraguan civil war, it stopped Israel from arming the Somoza government on retransfer prohibition grounds. The sale of six super-Mystère fighter bombers with U.S. engines to Honduras was also stalled, and until recently the Israeli-manufactured Kfir fighter-bomber could not be exported because it contained the U.S. J-79 engine. The Swedes have experienced similar restraints. In 1978, the United States was able to exercise a veto over the sale to India of the Viggen jet fighters because of their U.S. engines and components. "Arms Sales Reportedly Curbed," *Boston Globe*, August 26, 1979, p. 20; Graham Hovey, *New York Times*, January 15, 1977; "U.S. Vetoes Swedish jet sale to India," *Colorado Springs Sun*, August 15, 1978.

57. "Grounded at U.K.'s Request, U.S. Steps In To Block Israeli Sale of Jets to Argentina," *Defense Week* (August 26, 1985), 2; MILAVNEWS, February 1986.

58. Mary Acland-Hood, "Statistics on military research and development expenditure," *SIPRI Yearbook, 1984*, pp. 165–174.

59. "Special Report," *Defense Electronics* (May 1979), 58. French aircraft, which reputedly carry few U.S. components, are judged to be less capable than their U.S. counterparts. In 1978, one evaluation of the French Mirage F-1 was that "it didn't have many of the sophisticated electronic and control features that are needed to score air victories today." Beau Morris, "Why France's Arms Exports Make It a Paper Tiger," 19. For other discussions of the U.S. comparative production advantage, see Paul Lewis, *New York Times*, November 13, 1979; "Special Report," *Defense Electronics*; Stephanie G. Neuman, "The Arms Trade and American National Interest," in *Power and Policy in Transition*, 147–182.

60. Interview with U.S. industry official, February 1984.

61. Karen DeYoung, *Washington Post*, September 15, 1985;

Bernard Gwertzman, *New York Times*, September 16, 1985. For a more complete description of this sale, see Anthony Sampson, *The Arms Bazaar: From Lebanon to Lockheed* (New York: Viking Press, 1977), 157–164.

62. Sampson, *The Arms Bazaar*, 164.

63. Bernard Gwertzman, *New York Times*, September 16, 1985. See also "Britain to Sell Saudis 132 aircraft; France in deal with Iraq on Mirages," *Jewish Week*, October 11, 1985.

64. Quoted in "Saudis Set to Buy British Jets," *Washington Post*, September 15, 1985.

Index

Afghanistan: diversification and indirect supply, 51–52; human factors in, 80–84; Soviet military assistance to, 13, 17, 33, 80–81; Soviet support services for, 27–30; training in, 57, 81. *See also* Afghan rebels

Afghan rebels: cottage defense industry of, 39, 82; diversification and indirect supply, 51–52, 118; financial constraints on, 104–5; human factors and, 82–84; training of, 56, 59. *See also* Afghanistan

Africa, postwar resupply of, 19

age of weapons supplies, 20

aggression, prewar inventories and, 30

aircraft, Eastern vs. Western supplies of, 20

air force: Afghani, 81; Argentine, 62, 87–88; Iraqi vs. Iranian, 75; Israeli vs. Syrian, 67–68; PRC vs. Vietnamese, 64; Salvadoran, 79; Somali, 78

airlift capability, Soviet, 16

AK–47 Kalashnikov rifles, 81, 82–83

Algeria: financial assistance to the Polisario, 104; military assistance to Polisario, 51

AN–22 transport, 16

AN–400 transport, 16

antitank weapons, 66

Arab states, 49, 99. *See also individual states*

Argentina: as aggressor, 31; diversification of arms supply, 14, 47–48; diversified weapons procurement, 14; indigenous defense industries in, 3, 62–63, 70; military assistance to Contras, 50; and Soviet intelligence, 112; and training of insurgents, 58. *See also* Falklands war

Asia, postwar resupply of, 19

Austria, 122

battles: for the city of Harar, 77–78; of the Hawizah marshes, 75

Bayh, Birch, 82

bilateral arms agreements, 3–6; prewar/wartime patterns of, 9–15; U.S.-Soviet differences, 15–31; U.S.-